On Operations with C Squadron SAS

Also by Michael Graham:
Secret SAS Missions in Africa. C Squadron operations 1968 to 1980
Pen & Sword, 2017

SAS Action in Africa. C Squadron operations 1968 to 1980
Pen & Sword, 2019

On Operations with C Squadron SAS

Terrorist Pursuit and Rebel Attacks in Cold War Africa

Michael Graham

Pen & Sword

MILITARY

AN IMPRINT OF PEN & SWORD BOOKS LTD.
YORKSHIRE - PHILADELPHIA

First published in Great Britain in 2020 by
Pen & Sword Military
An imprint of
Pen & Sword Books Ltd
Yorkshire – Philadelphia

Printed and bound in the UK by TJ International Ltd, Padstow, Cornwall.

Pen & Sword Books Limited incorporates the imprints of Atlas, Archaeology, Aviation,
Discovery, Family History, Fiction, History, Maritime, Military, Military Classics,
Politics, Select, Transport, True Crime, Air World, Frontline Publishing, Leo Cooper,
Remember When, Seaforth Publishing, The Praetorian Press, Wharncliffe Local
History, Wharncliffe Transport, Wharncliffe True Crime and White Owl.

For a complete list of Pen & Sword titles please contact

PEN & SWORD BOOKS LIMITED
47 Church Street, Barnsley, South Yorkshire, S70 2AS, England
E-mail: enquiries@pen-and-sword.co.uk
Website: www.pen-and-sword.co.uk

Or
PEN AND SWORD BOOKS
1950 Lawrence Rd, Havertown, PA 19083, USA
E-mail: Uspen-and-sword@casematepublishers.com
Website: www.penandswordbooks.com

Contents

Author's Notes and Acknowledgements

In this third and final book my objective was to share some stories of the early days of C Squadron SAS, pay tribute to the few men who kept the unit alive after the break-up of the Federation of the Rhodesias and Nyasaland, and then to describe how our brigadier went on to rebuild it into an incredible fighting force that mastered the bush environment of Africa.

There were some interesting operations with the Portuguese in those early days. Through Central Intelligence Organisation leader Ken Flower, we learned of secret political alliances, and our covert involvement would have strengthened those relationships.

Secret SAS Missions in Africa and the sequel *SAS Action in Africa* describe the various operations the SAS were involved in until the end in 1980. At that point the British government had washed their hands of us and communist backed Mugabe was in power in our country.

The situation was untenable for us and the regiment was disbanded.

I am grateful for a man I don't know, called Kevin, in England, sending me copies of correspondence between our SAS General – the first commander of C Squadron SAS in Malaya – and Margaret Thatcher – the British Prime Minister. It is an interesting insight into high level politics that few of us mere mortals ever get to see, but it didn't change anything.

However, just because the regiment was disbanded the SAS story didn't end in 1980.

A large number of C Squadron members decided to go south and join the newly formed South African Special Forces known as the 'Recce Commando'. Most of the SAS had left by 1986, but not before involvement in operations that were not only dangerous, but destructive and even disastrous.

The SAS action in Africa thus continued for another six years.

I was half way through the writing of this book when I, the SAS Major who believed he was bulletproof, suddenly discovered he wasn't at all.

One day I was happily walking the hilly bush tracks in our lovely suburb of Titirangi in Auckland with my wife Sharen, and mowing the lawns thereafter.

Seventy-two hours later I was in the local hospital having 4½ litres of fluid drained from my lung cavity.

Thirty-six hours later I was having lung surgery and another 1½ litres of fluid were drained from the pleura.

I was told I had cancer.

No treatment options available and I had six months – maybe a bit a longer – to live on planet earth.

The first half of my remaining time they said would be OK and we were told to make the most of it, because the second part would see me with ever increasing tiredness and ever decreasing energy.

Sharen and I were pragmatic about it.

No point dwelling on the millions of disappointments this news brought us.

Far better to spend what time remained for me by seeing people we loved and going to our special places in New Zealand.

But on top of that there were dozens of personal details to get sorted which we managed OK and promptly.

My wonderful brother Andy organised a lawn mowing contractor to come every second week to do our extensive lawns, and that took away what was one of the major stress points for me with the bad news.

And the second point that stressed me was finishing SAS book three.

Did I have enough time?

I ploughed on through the chapters and have to say it was a welcome distraction from the seriousness of my medical situation. I soon realised I would finish the work, but editing by Caroline who had served me so well with the first two books would take too long.

I explained this to Caroline who was disappointed but understanding, and told me to send her the chapters anyway so she could read and comment on them. In Caroline I have been blessed with a great editor, and my life has been the richer for her involvement in it.

I turned to Henry Wilson for advice.

Henry is publishing editor for Pen and Sword who have been good enough to publish my writing, and we had met in London over a jolly good lunch at the Army & Navy Club. With both of us ex-Army it was not hard to get on well and we have enjoyed the relationship ever since.

I explained my medical situation to Henry who immediately told me to send the manuscript directly to him and they would do the editing.

He said that very few of his authors used a professional editor like Caroline, and the resultant quality of my manuscripts meant they had very little to do to turn it into a book. Barnaby Blacker, Pen & Sword's editor, was always so positive about my manuscripts so it was very pleasing to learn he would do the editing job.

So, thanks to Henry, the only other real stress this medical news brought was replaced with a positive and exciting situation as we debated titles, and Caroline came in with comments like the chapter about the assassination of Samora Machel was 'simply extraordinary'.

I hope the readers agree. It was an extraordinary story.

Pen & Sword Production Manager Matt Jones and jacket design wizard Jon Wilkinson, based in Barnsley, Yorkshire, deserve special praise. Two terrific guys who do a terrific job and I was so pleased to meet them when I visited Pen & Sword in 2017. Thank you both for making my books look so good.

God Bless you all.
Mike Graham
Auckland
April 2019

Profiles

The SAS General – Peter George Walls

Peter Walls was born in Salisbury, Southern Rhodesia, in 1927. His father was a First World War pilot who served with the Royal Air Force, and his son was set on a military career from the outset.

In 1945 he joined the British Army and was sent to Sandhurst for officer training. He received his commission in March 1946 and was posted to the Black Watch Regiment.

After a few years with the Black Watch, home was calling, and Peter returned to Africa to join the Rhodesian Army.

In 1951 he was promoted to Captain and became the first commander of what was to become C Squadron SAS. He led the SAS well in Malaya, was promoted to Major, and decorated with an MBE in 1953.

At the end of the campaign in Malaya he continued to make good progress in the Rhodesian Army. He attended Staff College in England in 1963, and by the time I joined the army in 1967 he was a Brigadier.

I met him in person for the first time in 1969 when he came out to do an early morning parachute jump with us. I was first in the stick and offered him my position. 'No, you lead the way, Mick,' he said. 'Today I'm just one of the boys.'

He was by then a Major General and Army Commander.

In 1972 I was appointed Military Intelligence Office to the brigade he'd commanded. The brigade deployed into the field at what was the real start of the Rhodesian bush war. Visits by ComOps became regular occurrences, and it was clear to everyone that amongst the other service chiefs Peter Walls was the natural leader.

This de facto status was formalised in 1977 when he was promoted to Lieutenant General with the title of Commander in Chief, and Head of the Rhodesian Armed Forces.

He left Zimbabwe in 1980 and lived a more peaceful life with his wife Eunice in the Western Cape until his death in July 2010.

CIO Chief Ken Flower

Ken Flower was born in Cornwall, England. With little prospect of employment in the deep depression of England in the 1930s, Ken responded to an ad in the *Daily Telegraph* looking for people to join the British South Africa Police in Southern Rhodesia.

Summoned to an interview in London Ken was dismayed to learn another 2,000 hopefuls had applied, but the interviewer picked up on the fact that Ken was a capable rugby player, representing Cornwall in the position of scrum half.

The BSAP team was desperately short of a scrum half, and in March 1937 Ken found himself on a ship bound for Africa.

After war service in Ethiopia and Somaliland Ken resumed police duties in Southern Rhodesia. He did well and promotions followed. By 1961 he was Deputy Commissioner of the BSAP.

In 1962 he was approached by Prime Minister Sir Winston Field who wanted him to form and head a national intelligence service – the CIO – Central Intelligence Organisation.

Ken Flower was a good choice for this position. He had allegiance with the British government, specifically with friends in MI6, and above all he saw himself as non-political.

His job was to obtain and analyse the intelligence, then present the findings dispassionately to his political masters, regardless of them liking the news or not. Ken Flower was a very talented analyst, but it was his dispassionate approach that earned him great respect and allowed him to successfully serve three different political regimes, including Robert Mugabe's at the end.

I got to know Ken Flower at the same time as General Walls as he was part of the ComOps team that visited us for updated field briefings. He and the General were the two stand-out personalities.

Ken enjoyed the SAS. He liked our professionalism and discretion, and later recruited two SAS men – Dudley Coventry and Danny Hartman – into his team.

The Brigadier – Peter Tremain

Born in Bury St Edmonds in the south-east of England, Peter was the youngest son in a family that was part of the Tate and Lyle dynasty that owned the local sugar beet refinery. After a public school education he graduated from the Royal Military Academy Sandhurst and was posted to the Argyll and Sutherland Highlanders.

Peter moved from his training role with 22 SAS, in Hereford, to take over command of C Squadron in the early days of our bush warfare campaign in Africa. He had seen action in Korea and in Malaysia, and then later on he was one of a small number of covert operators whose job, in the event of war, was to infiltrate behind East German and Russian lines and locate the assembly areas of armoured divisions preparing to advance. Once they had found a target, they would radio back the details and location and then it was 'Goodnight nurse' as he put it, because within minutes a missile with a tactical nuclear warhead would be launched and on its way.

There would be no escape option for the SAS men who delivered the critical information, and they were not expected to make it home – which goes to prove suicide bombers have been around for a while and are not exclusively Muslim.

Peter's immense experience combined with a razor-sharp mind and his laid-back leadership style generated huge respect.

He made us proud to be SAS and we'd do anything for him.

He was the perfect choice as our SAS leader.

After C Squadron SAS was disbanded Peter returned to England and became part of MI5. In January 1982 he was given a job in Spain and had planned on taking the train to Heathrow. However, British Rail decided to go on strike for more pay so he had to drive. There was bitterly cold weather over the UK at the time and road conditions were hazardous.

His car was hit from behind by another vehicle that lost control, probably on ice. His car was propelled over the median barrier and crashed head-on into a truck. Peter was killed instantly.

Peter was my first boss in the Rhodesian Light Infantry commandos, he was my boss in the SAS, he was my best man, and forever one of my greatest friends.

He was in many ways an eccentric, but never affected any airs and graces. He spoke his mind to Second Lieutenants and to Prime Ministers alike.

He was by far the most honest person I have ever met, but this didn't always win him friends. Senior officers and politicians didn't always like to hear the truth, especially if it conflicted with their own interests. Peter didn't compromise on this and was universally respected for his integrity.

Peter rates as one of the really great people I have known, and his death was a heavy burden to bear.

The Major – Mike (Mick) Graham

Mike was born in Burnley, on the Lancashire side of the northern moors in England, but raised in Rhodesia where his father was an instructor at an agricultural college with 350 students. A life-long interest in birdlife started when he was 10 years old and from this early age happiness was wandering across the 6,500 acres of college farm and woodland with his pointer dog companion.

After school Mike went to university in Natal, South Africa, where he studied zoology and botany with a dream of becoming a game ranger.

Called up for national service in Rhodesia, he enjoyed the army environment from the outset. He was commissioned as an officer and served in a commando unit before applying for SAS selection. He was duly awarded his wings and admitted to this elite unit.

After a number of years as a troop commander he was promoted to captain and posted to the position of intelligence officer at an operational brigade headquarters.

It was a turning point in his career. The job required close cooperation with senior officers in all the military branches as well as the air force, police and civil authorities and sometimes politicians. Mike made a mark and was decorated for his contribution.

Military staff college followed and a year later he graduated in the top three of his class.

He returned to the SAS as major and second in command of the regiment.

Vital statistics: height 1.8 metres (5 feet 11 inches); weight 82 kilograms (180 pounds).

Rex – Warrant Officer Rex Pretorius

Born in Pietersburg in the Northern Transvaal, South Africa, but raised on a massive 250,000-acre game ranch in the southern Matabeleland province of Rhodesia, Rex had a traditional Afrikaans family upbringing with a focus on hunting and living off the land. As a result he developed an environmental awareness akin to the animals they farmed and hunted.

He became a proficient mechanic and spent hours working on the open-top, short-wheel-base Land Rover that was the love of his life.

A big, powerful man, Rex worked as a professional hunter on another huge game ranch in the low veld of the Limpopo province before being called up to do national service in the army. His professional hunting work was seasonal and like the Major he too was attracted to the SAS and predictably had no problem with the selection course.

Rex led two lives, the first with the SAS and the second as a professional hunter. R and R for him was being reunited with his beloved Land Rover and going hunting. He was a true bushman.

Vital statistics: height 1.95 metres (6 feet 5 inches); weight 105 kilograms (230 pounds).

Karate – Sergeant Tony Caruthers Smith

Born in Bulawayo, Rhodesia, Karate, as he later became known, lost his father in a road accident when very young and was brought up by his mother who worked with the education department. He had a good academic record at school and was interested in electronics but had no specific career ambition.

Called up for national service with the army, which he enjoyed, Karate became a skilled radio operator. After joining the SAS, he took this to new levels with his mastery of Morse code and an uncanny knack of knowing just how to set up an aerial to ensure communications.

Karate and the Major were on the same advanced demolitions course and the two subsequently worked together on many operations involving the use of explosives. They were especially known for their skill in the tricky business of melting down Pentolite and moulding it into deadly 'bunker bombs' – family-sized plastic Coke bottles filled with the high explosive that were used to great effect on many occasions.

Karate had a cool head: relaxed when laying charges, calm under fire, and calculated and proactive during crises.

His slight stature and crooked, toothy grin disguised a hard, sinewy frame and tireless stamina. This physical strength combined with his mental resilience and technical skills made Karate one of Sierra One Seven's vital assets.

Vital statistics: height 1.725 metres (5 feet 8 inches); weight 75 kilograms (165 pounds).

Jonny – Corporal Jonasi Koruvakaturanga

Jonny was born in Lambasa, Fiji, the son of a ratu (tribal prince) who was general manager of the local sugar mill. He did his initial military training in Fiji and then joined the New Zealand army, serving in an infantry unit. Jonny heard about C Squadron through Pig Dog and joined him in the adventure to Africa.

Tall and with massive strength and stamina, Jonny was known as the best MAG gunner in the regiment and handled the heavy weapon as if it were an air rifle. Working in small numbers as we usually did, we relied massively on Horse and Jonny who carried the firepower in our group.

Vital statistics: height 1.95 metres (6 feet 5 inches); weight 106 kilograms (233 pounds), but nimble and quick with it.

Pig Dog – Corporal Verne Conchie

He was born in Riverton in Southland, New Zealand, of part-Maori parents. The family owned a deer farm on the narrow wind-blown plain at the southern extremity of the South Island, between the tumultuous seas of the Foveaux Strait and the impassable inland peaks of Fiordland.

By the age of ten Verne was hunting red deer and wild pigs alongside his father. They fished the streams together, put pots out for crayfish and collected shellfish. They would drive feral goats onto their property from neighbouring forests and either milked them to make cheese or slaughtered them for the Halal market.

Vern walked out of school at the age of 14 and initially worked full-time with his father before moving on as a deer hunter and seasonal hand at the local meat works. He was good at his job and managed to send a useful monthly contribution back home to his parents.

At the meat works he met Des and Amy Coles – an older man-and-wife team who had met while serving in the army together, and both saw the potential in Verne as a soldier. Des, who had been a regimental sergeant major, still had plenty of connections in the army and it wasn't long before he had talked Verne into giving it a try. The New Zealand SAS was on a recruiting drive at the time; Verne took up the challenge and thrived in the environment.

Vietnam was over and a chance to serve with an operational SAS regiment was there for the taking: the Kiwi found himself in Africa.

The name 'Pig Dog' has its origin in New Zealand where wild pigs are hunted with insanely tough breeds of dog that can have a gentle side to them. Bull terrier and bull mastiff crosses are popular. Verne looked a bit like a pig dog, he was built like a pig dog, and he had the strength and determination of a pig dog.

Verne Conchie was also incredibly loyal and devoted. We all knew he would put his body on the line for his comrades without any hesitation or consideration for his own safety. And with bush skills that rivalled Rex the two were an invincible lead-scout pairing with an instinct for danger that could not be taught.

Pig Dog was a legend!

Vital statistics: height 1.75 metres (5 feet 9 inches); weight 86 kilograms (190 pounds).

Fish – Corporal Paul Fisher

Paul was born in Ndola, Zambia, where his father was manager of a large copper mine. A combination of falling copper prices and political corruption disrupted the economy and the family moved to Rhodesia.

Paul had a good education and did well at school. Not a great sportsman, and branded an academic for no reason other than he wore glasses, he was determined to prove that physically he could hack it with the best of them. No better place to do that than with the SAS, and Paul was exceptional. He announced one day that what he particularly liked about the SAS was that in spite of all the heavy physical stuff demanded we were 'Soldiers who used our brains!' Amen to that. 'Fish', as we called him, used his brains to enrol for every course going, but discovered a special skill as a paramedic and the SAS subsequently channelled his focus on that.

When not on operations, he'd work as a male nurse at the local hospital accident and emergency ward.

Vital statistics: height 1.77 metres (5 feet 10 inches); weight 80 kilograms (175 pounds).

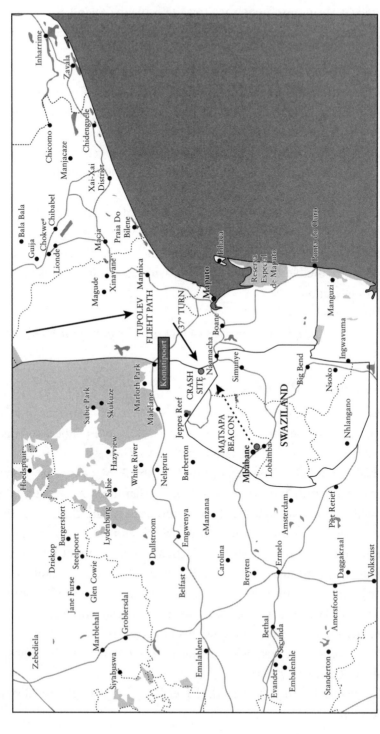

Map 1 – The late stages of the Tupolev Tu-134 flight path that crashed and killed Frelimo leader Samora Machel.

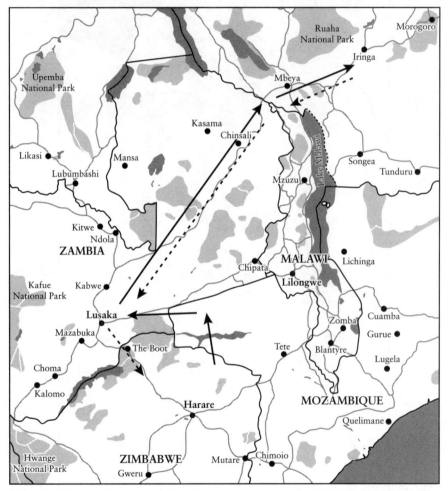

Map 2 – Henry Munyaradzi's travels and where the SAS found his boot.

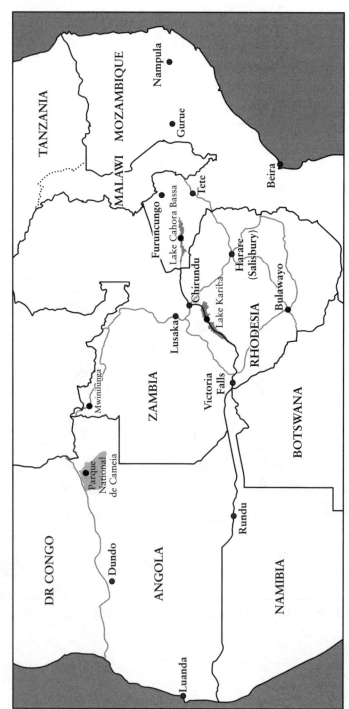

Map 3 – Map used previously to show SAS operational area, but with additions to Angola and Mozambique.

Rebirth of the SAS – 1952

After the Second World War the original SAS was disbanded. A communist uprising in South East Asia prompted its re-establishment with help from Commonwealth countries:

British Army — 22 SAS Squadron

A Squadron – England
B Squadron – England
C Squadron – Rhodesia – Mike Graham
D Squadron – Scotland

Australian Army — Australian SAS

New Zealand Army — NZSAS

C Squadron SAS

While Mao Tse-Tung was fighting the Japanese in China during 1944, the Malayan National Liberation Army (MNLA) was doing the same on the northern border of Malaya.

Secretly trained and armed by the British, the MNLA was the military wing of the Malayan Communist Party (MCP) whose support was based on around 500,000 of the 3.12 million ethnic Chinese then living in Malaya.

The MNLA was disbanded in December 1945 and members were offered cash incentives to hand their weapons back to the British – $1,000 for a Bren Gun for example. Many took advantage of the reward system but at least 4,000 of them wanted nothing to do with it and went underground.

There were several reasons for this.

The main reason at the start would have been desperation. The Japanese invasion and the cost of war had completely disrupted the economy of the country, that had been based on revenue from tin mines and rubber plantations.

There was mass unemployment, low wages, food was scarce and inflated in price, and the basic infrastructure of the country was a shambles.

At the same time the power and influence of Mao Tse-Tung and his communist doctrine had increased dramatically. He'd chased Chiang Kai-shek and his National Government of China out of the country and into exile in Taiwan. In its place Mao formed the People's Republic of China and encouragingly pledged alliance with the communist parties of Vietnam, Korea and Malaya.

And finally, there was the thorny issue of ethnicity.

The Chinese in Malaya were regarded as squatters. They were denied the equal right to vote in elections, they had no land rights, and generally were very poor. And that's the way the ethnic Malayans wanted to keep it. Malaya was for Malayans. It would never be taken over by the Chinese.

In protest the MCP organised a series of protracted strikes that took place between 1946 and 1948. During this time, the British colonial administration was trying to reorganize the economy, as revenue from the tin mines and rubber plantations was important to its own post-war recovery.

As a consequence, the striking protesters were dealt with harshly.

During my own officer training many years later I well remember a series of films made by the British Army called 'Keeping the Peace'. Part two showed how to deal with urban protests and much of it was filmed in Malaya.

None of us who saw the films will ever forget the famous lines as the riot spiralled out of control: 'Two Platoon. One round at the man in the red shirt. Fire!!!!!!'

And that's what they did.

At 0830 hrs on 16 June 1948 the MCP fired back.

Three British plantation managers were executed in Perak, the coastal province between Kuala Lumpur and Penang.

The British Administration responded by declaring a state of emergency, the MCP was outlawed, and the police were given power to detain communists and those suspected of supporting them.

The MCP, led at the time by Chin Peng, retreated back to the jungle fringes where they had fought the Japanese and where most of the Chinese squatter population lived. They immediately recreated the MNLA and began a guerrilla offensive, mainly targeting the colonial-controlled tin mines and rubber plantations.

In June 1948 the MNLA attacked and occupied the small railway town of Gua Musang, situated in deep jungle on the northern border of the famous Taman Negara National Park. The Malayan Emergency had started in earnest.

The guerrillas were well received by the locals and many joined the cause. Their hideouts and camps were located in inaccessible jungle, and they were surrounded by sympathizers who supplied food and intelligence.

Their numbers increased and they followed Mao's teachings of staying in small groups, moving far and wide, never staying in one place too long, and after a strike disappearing back into the jungle or amongst the mass of the population – 'like the fishes in the sea' as he put it so well.

At first the security forces didn't know how to fight an enemy moving freely in the jungle and enjoying support from the Chinese rural population. They tried large formation sweeps that were both clumsy and complete failures.

Then in October 1951 the British High Commissioner in Malaya, Sir Henry Gurney, was assassinated by a guerrilla band.

It was time for a rethink and a change of command.

Amongst a number of changes made by the British were two that turned out to be pivotal in ultimately achieving victory.

The first of these was General Gerald Templer who was appointed British High Commissioner and later credited for turning the fortunes of war in favour of the British forces. His particular contribution was embarking on a 'hearts and minds' campaign, using troops to distribute food and medical aid to Malays and other indigenous tribes.

At the same time Sir Robert Grainger Ker Thompson was made Permanent Secretary for Defence for Malaya. The significance of this appointment was that he had served with Orde Wingate's Chindits in Burma.

The Chindits were an irregular unit that attacked Japanese troops, facilities and lines of communication deep behind Japanese lines.

With this background he realised that troops trained and experienced in jungle warfare were best suited to counter the guerrilla offensive. They would patrol and ambush the rivers and jungle, forcing the guerrillas deeper and deeper into the jungle and away from the population that was supporting them.

To make this happen he enlisted the support of Brigadier Mike Calvert who had been one of the Chindit commanders.

Calvert was put in charge of forming the Malayan Scouts, that were ultimately to become 22 SAS.

He firstly formed A Squadron from English troops; B Squadron was formed from an English SAS territorial force that had operated in Korea but was about to be disbanded, and then he went on a recruiting campaign to Rhodesia.

Serving in the Long Range Desert Group and in the original SAS, Rhodesians had shown they were good special forces material. It was this background, an inherent willingness to support Britain, and Mike Calvert's reputation and character that persuaded the Rhodesian government of the day to fund a force of 100 volunteers.

C Squadron SAS was born.

For those founder members of C Squadron, the emergency in Malaya consisted of a lot of patrolling in heat and high humidity and not a lot of action.

It was the same for everyone.

Operation Nissau began in January 1955. Its objective was to eliminate a guerrilla group based in an extensive swamp area.

At first the swamp was bombed and shelled day and night in the hope that the terrorists would be driven out into ambushes. When that didn't work the plan was modified with shelling limited to night-time only, while ambushes and patrols inside the swamp intensified. This continued for three months without results, until finally on 21 March an ambush killed two of eight terrorists in a group.

Another month passed before the next contact when a single terrorist was killed in an ambush.

Nothing happened for another two months until a patrol bumped into a terrorist group and accounted for one killed and one captured. Patrolling in that area intensified and another contact resulted in two terrorists killed.

In July the patrols had found the leader's camp and in the attack four, including the leader, were killed. Other patrols accounted for four more. By the end of July, seven months later, just twenty-three terrorists remained in the swamp. They were cut off from the outside world and had no food.

Such was the nature of operations in Malaya.

Tallying it up afterwards, 60,000 artillery shells, 30,000 mortar bombs and 2,000 aircraft bombs were used on Operation Nissau for a return of 35 terrorists killed or captured. Each kill also represented 1,500 man-days of patrolling or waiting in ambush.

Operation Nassau was considered a success because the end of the campaign was one step nearer.

The conflict in Malaya involved some 40,000 British and Commonwealth troops up against some 8,000 communist fighters at peak strength.

1,865 allied troops were killed and 2,406 were wounded.

6,710 communists were killed, 1,289 were wounded, 1,287 were captured and 2,702 surrendered.

In excess of 5,000 civilians also died in the conflict.

C Squadron was relieved by the New Zealand SAS and returned to Africa.

They found themselves in what was then Northern Rhodesia, based in the copper mining town of Ndola and part of the armed forces of the Federation of Rhodesia and Nyasaland.

At the end of 1963 with independence granted to Northern Rhodesia (now Zambia) and Nyasaland (now Malawi) the Federation broke up. Members of C Squadron were given options for their future. They could either take what was known as 'The Golden Handshake' and go their own way, or they could head south to become part of the Rhodesian Army.

Just thirty-eight men decided to keep C Squadron alive and moved to Salisbury.

Recruitment from 1964 was slow at first but gathered momentum in 1968 when our brigadier took charge. He reinvigorated the unit with new officers and men. He put us all through an intensive six months retraining period, and then set operational standards that would ultimately transform C Squadron into highly professional bush warfare specialists.

C Squadron strength peaked at around 250 men in 1978 and they continued to serve with outstanding success and distinction across the countries of central Africa until the unit was disbanded in 1980.

Rebuilding

Until Pen & Sword Books used the full Christian name of 'Michael' on my first title the only other person on earth to have called me that was my mother. Mum and Dad were Lancashire folk from Burnley and although they ended up living most of their lives in Africa they never lost their accents. So, to my mother I was 'our Michael', which is quite endearing, but everyone else – my father and two sisters, all my primary and senior school friends and new friends I later made at university in South Africa – called me 'Mike'.

In spite of studying zoology at university I had no idea there was an animal on earth known as an 'Army Officer' until 1967 when I found myself on a training course aimed at making me one.

But there was a problem.

There was another 'Mike' on the training course.

'That's no bloody use,' said training officer Lieutenant Charlie Aust as he picked out a coin from his wallet.

'Heads Mike. Tails Mick,' he said tossing the coin in the air.

I lost the toss and for the thirteen years that followed I was 'Mick Graham'.

The SAS, the whole of the Rhodesian Army, the Rhodesian Airforce, Police, Special Branch, Internal Affairs and the odd politician we mixed with all knew me as 'Mick' and I wasn't at all unhappy about it.

The Brigadier hadn't long been in command of C Squadron when I got my wings and he wasn't happy.

In his view the regiment had stagnated, it had become cliquey and he wasn't impressed with an arrogant attitude that didn't match the actual standards he was seeing. The Brigadier was a laid-back character and encouraged everyone to be the same, but that approach only works when you are dealing with polished professionals, so he set about putting that right.

He called me into his office one afternoon and explained things to me.

'Mick,' he said, 'I'm just about to go to a meeting with the general. I am going to ask him to excuse us from all operational duties for the next six months. I'm going to get this unit back into shape with some leadership changes and a period of intensive retraining.

'We need some more young officers and new blood in the ranks. I want you to join Ken Philipson and scour the country for suitable SAS material. Ken will look after the ranks; your job is to get me some officers.'

I saluted, wished him luck with the general, and went to find Ken – the SAS Training Officer.

Ken and I returned three weeks later after visiting military establishments in the main centres of Salisbury, Umtali, Gwelo and Bulawayo.

Ken rounded up over thirty volunteers and twenty-four of them went on to pass Selection Course and get their SAS wings. That was a great result and a tribute to Ken's eye for suitable material. Mathematically it was brilliant because it basically gave us another one and a half Troops – as each SAS Troop consisted of sixteen men.

I managed to talk Bert Sachse across from the tight-knit Rhodesian Light Infantry commando unit, and had more success with the Rhodesian African Rifles based in Bulawayo.

Ian McClean and I were school contemporaries. Ian had gone straight into the army after school and graduated as the top – Sword of Honour – officer cadet on his course so, as can be imagined, I was delighted to have him on side. Ian was also very helpful in getting Ian Moore, Howard Inman and Ron Marillier to join him, while I tracked down Rob Ford who had been with me on officer course; Rob also agreed to giving the SAS a go.

Ian Wardle decided his training job at the School of Infantry was too tame, and finally I used Pig Dog's influence to talk a great New Zealander into joining us. Martin Knight-Willis from the New Zealand SAS was decorated with a Military Cross in Vietnam and was a great asset to us from the outset – and a great personal friend to this day, I might add.

All the new officers breezed through selection and suddenly we had the experienced leadership talent the Brigadier was looking for. With three of the Rhodesian officers already wearing the Bronze Cross for gallantry and Martin's MC from Vietnam we had an officer pedigree the squadron hadn't seen before.

The Brigadier responded by reorganising the unit.

Troops became 'Sections' – so my original B Troop became 2 Section.

He then split the Squadron into two 'Troops' – A and B – each with four sections consisting of an officer, two sergeants and another thirteen men. To the troops he then added dedicated support staff – signallers, drivers, medics and storemen for example, along with all their equipment. The Troops thus became operationally independent.

It meant the SAS could now be deployed in strength in two different places at the same time, and as the conflicts in Central Africa escalated that is generally how we operated as a regiment. We only came together for exceptional assignments such as the attack on the massive ZANU base at Chimoio in Mozambique where we eliminated some 1,200 terrorists in November 1977.

The other effect the reorganisation had on the unit was to develop internal competition.

As the retraining progressed there were more and more competitions between sections and between the two troops. These included matches on the shooting range, physical tests on the assault course, or live firing tactical training exercises. Spurred on by the new officers and their invigorated sergeants it didn't take long before everyone wanted to be the winner – wanted to be the best.

And it worked.

In a few short months C Squadron was once again looking like what one would expect of an SAS regiment.

At the same time the Brigadier beefed up our intelligence personnel and equipment.

We ended up with an Operations Theatre with comprehensive regional map coverage, air photography viewing units and, in the centre, a large floor space where the intelligence team built some amazing cloth models either to exercise us or to prepare us for an operation. The entire regiment could be seated on stands around these models. The Brigadier would be on the floor, centre stage. The ringmaster in total command.

His presence and personality were such that he always had everyone's undivided attention, but he made absolutely sure of that with an unnerving habit of suddenly popping a question to the audience, and it could be directed at anyone, regardless of rank.

It was very skilful management on his part. It made these briefings totally inclusive. Everybody was involved and as we got used to his style and became more confident the level of participation increased. It was exactly what the Brigadier wanted. He wanted us to challenge him with comment, ideas or thoughts on what might be a better way. And if an idea or suggestion put forward from the floor had merit there would be no hesitation in adopting it in the plan.

With this level of involvement, it should come as no surprise to learn that we seldom had operational cock-ups. Inevitably there were a few mishaps, sometimes external forces – like the weather – worked against us, and sometimes our plans didn't come off because for some reason the enemy simply didn't turn up.

Finally, the Brigadier also gave us our identity.

He explained how 22 SAS had specialists; some for countering hostage situations, others in dealing with hijacked aircraft. In C Squadron there were many of us who were completely at home in the African bush and used to sharing it with big game animals. He suggested we build on this; focussing on mastering the African bush environment and in so doing becoming the bush warfare elite.

And that's what happened.

C Squadron became an unknown invisible force that could strike anywhere. Our enemies had no idea they were up against the SAS and they had no answer to our tactics.

After twelve years of continuous operations it all came to an end.

In 1980 the unit was disbanded following Mugabe's seizure of power in Zimbabwe.

The end was messy and heart-breaking. Many of us, myself included, scattered to the four winds. A good number of others opted to join the South African special forces known as the 'Recce Commando'. For them the aftermath was war for another six years.

My right-hand man 'Karate' was one of the team who joined the Recce Commando. He later came out to New Zealand to see me and Pig Dog and told us his post-SAS story.

It was as if he'd never really left the SAS. His stories are included in this book in memory because Karate was tragically killed in an accident not long after seeing us.

For me 1980 was an extraordinary year.

The SAS was over and I'd got myself a proper job with Dunlop Engineering Group in England. There I met my New Zealand born wife Sharen and it wasn't long before I was offered the position of Auckland and Pacific Manager. In early December 1980 before leaving for New Zealand I went to say farewell to David Aire – the Dunlop director whom I'd met in Africa and who took me on.

I thanked him for everything he had done for me but before leaving said I had a question: 'When we first met I was introduced to you as 'Mick Graham' but on arrival in England and without any prompting on my part everyone called me 'Mike'. Why is that David?' I asked.

'Couldn't possibly call you Mick old boy,' he replied. 'Mick's a bloody Irish ditch digger.'

In late-December 1980 I became a Kiwi – and I got my name back!

Escape and Evasion

The Brigadier had ordered the whole squadron to a meeting in the Operations Room at 1000 hours. He'd not ordered any specific seating as he usually did, so we randomly filled up the stands around the centre of the room where normally a cloth model would have been constructed.

We all stood up and braced when he walked in, and to our surprise he was followed by an Air Force Wing Commander and two pilots most of us knew. One flew a Hunter jet and the other was a helicopter jockey. The Air Force men took seats in the front row while the Brigadier walked into the centre of our SAS stage.

'I am very pleased with the results of our training courses and exercises,' he began, 'and three weeks today we will be returning to operational duties. We will be deploying into the lower Zambezi Valley where for six weeks we will conduct border control and a number of cross border reconnaissance operations. Although operational I want you all to regard this forthcoming deployment as on-going training towards our goal of being recognised as the bush warfare elite force.

'In the remaining time of our retraining period I have decided to run an exercise in which you all will be involved; but for some, the test will be much greater.'

He paused and dug into a pocket while we all watched in complete silence.

In his hand he held a small tinfoil capsule. He held it above his head and walked around the stands so we could all get a good look at what he was holding.

'A few of you here will already know what this is. It is a cyanide suicide tablet.'

There were murmurs and nervous shuffling of feet as he circled the room.

'These tablets were developed in world war two for special operatives but were also used by the Nazi hierarchy. Hitler took one then also shot himself. Göring, Bormann, Himmler and Rommel all took their own lives with these tablets.

'There are three scenarios for the use of the tablet. The first and most obvious is to avoid capture and the likely torture and possible execution that would go with it. The second, which in my view is more compelling, is to avoid capture so as not to give the enemy crucial operational or technical intelligence.

'But the most compelling reason of all is to avoid capture so as not to compromise the safety of your comrades, and it is this that will be tested in the exercise.

'I have selected twenty of you to be fugitives on Exercise Pipeline – an escape and evasion exercise that will start tomorrow in the Eastern districts. Because the SAS are not the only ones facing the possibility of capture inside unfriendly territory I have invited the Air Force to participate. They have nominated two of their pilots who will join the fugitive band.

'The exercise will commence with the fugitives managing to escape while being transported. They will have nothing other than their clothes. They will each be given details of a rendezvous some distance away where a friendly agent will give them food and directions to the next rendezvous in the pipeline heading towards the border and freedom.

'As soon as the escape of the fugitives is reported the remainder of you will join the local police in a manhunt to track down and recapture the escapees. The Air Force are providing helicopter support to assist in the search and also to be on hand for any casevac requirements.

'An Interrogation Centre will be set up at the Umtali Showgrounds and we have put together a team of experienced interrogators including a psychologist used by the South African Defence Forces. Their role in the event of a capture is to obtain the detail of the next rendezvous in the pipeline so our forces can intercept more of the fleeing fugitives.

'You will be pleased to know that I won't be issuing the cyanide pills and anyone captured won't be executed. Those caught will however be subject to an intense interrogation that will not be pleasant. It will be something none of you have previously experienced and will be a rigorous test of your mental fortitude. It will be very interesting to see how you cope.

'The location of the agents given to the fugitives will be valid for just 36 hours. If that information can be withheld from the interrogators for

36 hours it will thereafter be of little value to the pursuit teams, and those still at large will not be compromised. Resisting for 36 hours is the basic challenge for those who get captured.

'And by the way,' he added with a smile, 'those of us controlling the exercise will be doing our best to ensure most, if not all, of the fugitives are captured and interrogated.'

The Brigadier paused again as he pulled out a piece of paper from the map pocket on his camo trousers.

We all fidgeted nervously, most of us I'm sure hoping our names would not be on his list.

Personally I thought I would quite enjoy the challenge of the escape and evasion but didn't like the prospect of interrogation. Apart from anything else it was mid-winter and would be freezing cold. Anyway, the Brigadier knew me well enough by now. More likely some of the new officers would be his preference.

He unfolded the piece of paper and my name was the first he read out from the list.

The following afternoon the twenty of us and the two airmen reported to the Medical Room where we were strip-searched then put on a truck. We were all dressed in our usual camouflage gear with a warm camouflage jacket as the only luxury.

The truck stopped at a railway siding next to the concrete works on the outskirts of town. A few minutes later a freight train arrived and we were shepherded into an empty freight carriage with a wooden sliding door.

As we boarded we were each given a scrap of paper. On it was a rough sketch of where we would find the agent near a place known as 'Eagle's Nest'. There we would be given food and the next set of directions. A footnote said the agent would be at the rendezvous from 1600 to 2000 hours the following night.

Eagle's Nest was around one hundred kilometres away from the town of Umtali where the Brigadier had said they would be establishing the interrogation centre. In calling the exercise 'Pipeline' I assumed he would try to keep us running parallel with the road and rail links to the town. That would make sense in terms of deploying the pursuit teams and give them every chance of catching us.

We sat on the wooden floor of the carriage, leaning against the walls as the train chugged off into the night. It was cold and drafty inside the carriage so I put up the collar of my jacket, folded my arms and tried to sleep. I did manage to doze off for short spells but in between naps I was thinking about what to do once we were released.

I listened to the others talking amongst themselves.

Five decided to go as a group with just one risking the meeting with the agent while the others watched from cover. Not a bad idea I thought but not for me. I knew Rex and the other trackers in the squadron would have no difficulty following five sets of prints.

The airmen decided to go as a pair.

The others spoke of how they would run for some hours to get well clear of the drop-off point before the pursuit teams arrived. I liked that idea too but was still thinking about Rex and how he'd also run on the tracks as he followed them.

I decided that I would walk on the railway tracks through the night to get me well clear of the drop-off point and then I'd head off into the bush as daylight approached. Nobody had said anything about using dogs and only a dog could follow my scent trail along the railway line, that would also take me in the general direction of the first RV.

After a few hours the train stopped.

We heard African voices.

The sliding door of the carriage was suddenly opened.

Nothing happened and the voices had gone.

Realizing what this was about I leapt to my feet, jumped out of the train and started running towards the engine.

It was a long train and before I reached the front it had started to move again. I kept jogging alongside the tracks. I recognised our carriage with the open door as it passed me, and then there was just a red tail light slowly disappearing in the distance.

I kept running.

I was on my own with the SAS, Police and Air Force against me.

But they would have to be bloody good to catch me!

I kept up a good pace along the railway line for about four hours when suddenly the line branched and in front of me were buildings. I moved in a bit closer then knelt down to watch and listen.

Nothing.

It looked like the small siding was deserted.

I moved in for a closer look, realising this may be an opportunity for me to improve my situation, given I had nothing other than the clothes I was wearing.

On the platform there was a small open-sided shelter with a bench and behind it what looked like a garage.

I approached with caution.

Were people living there? Even worse, would there be dogs?

I stopped to watch and listen for a few minutes.

Again nothing, so I closed in for a better look.

There was a large sliding door securing the front of the garage but around the side I found a pedestrian door. I gingerly turned the door knob and applied gentle pressure. The hinges squeaked but to my delight the door opened and I went inside.

It was a workshop with a bench and many tools hanging on the wall and scattered around on the floor. I found a small knife on the bench and put that in my pocket. In the dark I groped across to a corner and there struck gold!

On top of a rusting steel cabinet was a kettle, a tin mug with a teaspoon, and a jar half full of tea bags. I swished the kettle around and could hear the swirl of water. I found the power plug and switched it on. A few minutes later I was enjoying a hot cup of tea with a big smile on my face.

I continued my search and had more luck. My groping hand knocked over a small item that rattled as it hit the floor. I recognised the sound. It was a box of matches. I could not have been happier.

I finished the tea, put the mug, spoon, tea bags and matches in my jacket pockets and went back on to the railway line.

As I walked I was thinking about how best to manage the RVs. I thought there would be little risk of compromise at this first one because it was very early in the exercise and we had a good start on the pursuit teams, but thereafter caution would be the order of the day.

I decided to risk running into the RV as soon as it opened at 1600hrs and again make haste away from the danger zone. After that however I decided I would stay in cover some distance away from the RVs and watch proceedings. If the coast looked clear I would leave the meeting until the last minute before again disappearing into the night.

The first RV was a breeze. I rushed down towards the bridge as my watch hit 1600hrs. Training Officer Ken Philipson greeted me and gave me a small brown paper bag. I grabbed it and jogged back towards the cover where I'd waited for the RV to open. I kept going fast in the remaining daylight, trying wherever I could to anti-track.

Rex and I had spent a lot of time together and I knew better than anyone how good he was at following tracks. I would have to be very careful.

Inside the paper bag was another rough sketch map showing the next RV, a raw carrot, three Star cigarettes with three matches, and an oat biscuit. I didn't smoke but thought I may be able to trade the cigarettes for food if along the way I found an African village.

That night I made a small fire, cut up the carrot and boiled it in my tin mug. I drank the juice and enjoyed the warm vegetable – hoping it would improve my night vision as some would have you believe.

At the second RV I sat in cover and watched.

Ken Philipson was standing next to a road sign holding some more brown paper bags. I saw the two airmen walk up towards him, followed by two of my SAS colleagues. As they approached, twenty concealed SAS men suddenly stood up and pointed their rifles at them. I watched as the runners were handcuffed to the rails on the back of the Sabre Land Rovers that drove away to the interrogation centre.

I continued observing until I saw Ken looking at his watch.

I ran down to him, grabbed a brown paper bag and without saying anything turned and ran back into the cover where I had waited.

The third RV I knew would be even more difficult. As part of the exercise team Ken would have told everyone how I had left making the RV until the very last minute. It was unfair but we had been warned they would be doing their very best to catch all of us.

I'd have to rethink my approach.

In the event I got lucky.

One of the other boys on the run managed to sneak up to one of the parked Land Rovers while the SAS group waited in ambush at the RV.

The keys were still in the ignition. He didn't need telling twice. He jumped into the driving seat, started up and roared off down the road.

He was seen by the ambush party who abandoned their positions and ran to the other vehicles to give pursuit. And while that was happening I made my way down to the RV and took another brown paper bag.

I ran out of luck at the fourth RV.

I again hid some distance away to observe proceedings. I watched as two runners were caught by an ambush group and taken away to the Land Rovers.

After the capture the troops spread out and started a wide sweep around the RV area. I was too far away to be worried about this but didn't dare move as the sweep progressed. I decided to abandon the RV and just take a guess at where the next one may be.

As the troops came closer I heard a bark and saw the shape of a long-haired dog leaping through the grass and cover ahead of the sweep line. It was a Red Setter and I knew the dog well. It belonged to one of the sergeants and I had looked after it for a month while he took his family on a holiday to South Africa.

It was the scattiest dog I'd ever met, but it was very affectionate and loved accompanying me on my bird watching walks.

I watched with apprehension as it stopped opposite where I was hiding, still a good distance away. I could see it testing the wind with its nose. And then to my horror it barked and came bounding towards me.

It didn't take long to find me. The Red Setter jumped on top of me, licking my neck, tail wagging and barking excitedly. I stood up and stroked the dog as it jumped up against my front.

'You little bastard,' I said as it barked again and tried to lick my face.

A few hours later I was at the Umtali showgrounds. It was dark and I was standing in a pigsty.

I'd been stripped and was then told to put on a pair of large black running shorts with the crotch cut out. A white hood made from some stiff material was put over my head. They put leg irons on me and my arms were held behind my back with handcuffs.

The pigsty was open at the front and while I was under cover I was to all intents and purposes totally exposed to the environment. It was freezing cold and my bare feet soon became numb on the cold concrete floor.

And I had to keep standing.

The handcuffs behind my back were attached to something that made it impossible for me to sit or lie down.

Then just to be sure I wasn't enjoying myself too much somebody came along and poured a bucket of cold water over my head.

I stood and shivered.

'How am I going to handle this?' I asked myself, desperate to find some direction. I couldn't just stand here and let my life be taken over. I had to find a distraction – something to cling to.

My first mental break was hearing an eagle owl grunting close to the pigsty.

I mimicked the call.

It called back.

Another bucket of cold water was thrown over me.

I stopped mimicking the call but the owl was still there and I listened.

My next mental break some hours later was thanks to Karate.

We'd all been given another dose of cold water.

I recognised his voice as he called out after his dousing.

'Hey Sarge,' he said, 'next time you come around would you mind washing down my arse? My top is pretty good now but my bum stinks.'

Laughter erupted from the pigsty and I realised there were a good number of us now captured.

Karate got his wish not long after as the water party returned and firstly poured a bucket of the freezing cold water down the front of his shorts, followed by another down his back. And for good measure the rest of us got another dose as well.

The night dragged by with only the odd water dousing to relieve the tedium of standing in the freezing cold of the pigsty.

I realised what game the interrogators were playing and there wasn't really anything I could do about it.

We were being deprived of sleep and at the same time being subjected to great physical discomfort. It was very cold and we had to keep standing – hour after long hour.

As a distraction I tried judging the time.

My guess, it was in the early hours of the morning when I got my next mental break.

In the pigsty next to me I heard another familiar voice.

It was a young sergeant I played rugby with. He was quite a talented player but we all noticed he was more than a little bit ginger when it came down to one on one physical contact. As a result, I never really trusted him and quietly made sure he wasn't ever part of my SAS operations.

'To hell with this!' I heard him call out. 'Dumb exercise. I want out of here.'

The guards immediately took him away and I felt like shouting out, 'You bloody wanker! You have just compromised the others still out there.'

I didn't say anything but I was boiling with anger. We didn't need weak willed pricks like that in the SAS. I hoped the brigadier would kick his arse into touch and we'd never see him again.

Having said that to myself I now couldn't possibly give in to the interrogators. I was determined I would resist long enough for my RV information to be worthless.

Getting angry like that was the best thing that happened to me on that long first night.

I heard the crowing of cockerels and knew first light was approaching.

They say the coldest part of the day is just before sunrise, and the guards made sure of that by dousing us all again with ice-cold water.

I shivered but mentally I was feeling good. I was now about a third of the way to the objective I had given myself. I wouldn't say a word for 36 hours.

We were told that under interrogation you only spoke your number, rank and name.

Bugger that I thought.

They will get nothing from me. I'm not going to say an effing word.

The sun had been up for a few hours and I was enjoying the warmth when the guards abruptly entered my pigsty and roughly grabbed me, one on each side. They hustled me across a gravel road that was uncomfortable on my feet. The leg irons hurt my ankles as I struggled to keep pace with the guards.

I was dragged up some concrete stairs, scraping and stubbing my toes on each step because the leg irons were too tight for me to reach them. A door opened and I was shoved into a dark room. For a minute or so I was left standing there wondering what the hell was happening.

I heard movement and suddenly a bright spotlight came on above my head.

My eyes were still getting used to the light when somebody came across to me and pulled off the hood. 'Number, rank and name!' he shouted in my face.

I squinted at the figure in front of me, still trying to see properly, but said nothing.

I could now see it was a man I didn't know. He was about my size and build. His face was so close it almost made contact and as he again shouted 'Number, rank and name!' I felt his spittle on my cheek.

Again, I said nothing.

He shouted again, and this time followed it by shoving me in the chest. I stepped back as far as I could with the leg irons to keep my balance, then bent my knees and lunged forward with all my strength.

The head butt hit him on the bridge of the nose. He cried out in pain and surprise while blood spurted everywhere.

He staggered towards me, his face covered in blood.

A big swinging fist hit me in the solar plexus, just beneath my sternum. I dropped to the ground, gasping to get my breath back. He came towards me and I was sure I was about to be kicked.

I curled up as if to protect myself from being kicked, but as he closed in my knees uncoiled like a released spring and with all the power I could muster the heels of both my feet smashed into his right knee cap.

There was another cry of surprise and pain as he dropped to the ground.

Suddenly voices were shouting 'Stop! Stop!'

The guards rushed in, grabbed my arms, pulled me up to my feet and put my hood back on. Adrenalin was still pumping through my veins but I realised further resistance would be futile. I took deep breaths and tried to calm myself mentally as my pulse and blood pressure slowly returned to normal.

Back in my pigsty I thought about what I'd just done.

I was pleased I hadn't said a word, and while hitting the interrogator was a good physical and mental respite I realised it would undoubtedly come at a cost. Nothing I could do about that now, I thought, but meanwhile another few hours had passed. The interrogators would know they were running out of time with me. The pressure had to intensify.

It started an hour or two later.

Alongside the road leading into the showgrounds was neatly trimmed grass with a line of evenly spaced white painted granite stones each the size of a bucket. The stones were chipped from bigger blocks and most had sharp, jagged edges.

Holding me by the arms the guards straddled the line of stones, and with me in the middle began a slow jog along the length of the roadway.

With my leg irons it was desperately painful just to keep up with them and with my hood on I had no way of telling where the stones were. By the time we reached the top of the road my feet were badly bruised, cut and bleeding.

The guards turned me round and we ran back over the stones.

In the pigsty I was in a lot of pain but had to keep standing on my feet. A water dousing would have been good, but that had stopped. I had to find some sort of distraction to keep me going mentally.

It came in the form of two small black ants.

I must have brushed a branch of one of the shrubs while stone walking with the guards and bumped the ants onto my hood. I didn't see them until they found their way to the inside.

They scurried up and down on the stiff cloth, running in erratic figures of eight. They worked their way up to eye level then changed their mind and direction, hurrying back towards the base of the hood. I thought it would have been easy for them to go back to the outside but for some reason they didn't.

I watched with amusement as they explored up, down and sideways, sometimes stopping to investigate something of interest – maybe a drop of my sweat – before resuming their eternal frantic search.

It rested my brain and I felt much better, but inevitably it wasn't to last.

The guards returned and initially took me for another stone walk before leading me into the darkened room with the interrogators.

Still holding each arm one of them took off my hood.

I was standing in front of a zinc dustbin that was full of water.

Without warning the two guards forced my head down and submerged it in the dustbin.

I tried to relax but panic was close as I ran out of breath and in the nick of time they lifted my head up.

I spluttered and coughed, and just managed a deep breath before once again my head was submerged.

This time I did relax, telling myself this was just an exercise and they were not going to drown me. I tried fooling them by blowing bubbles and struggling and at first it worked, but every time they lifted my head out of the water I seemed to have less time to take in the air I needed for the next dunking.

I was very thirsty when they took me into the room. But the last thing I wanted now was more water.

As I stood there panting, the interrogator, who now had a thick white plaster across the bridge of his nose, approached and demanded my number, rank and name. Sensibly he kept well clear of me while the guards maintained their hold.

'Eff you,' I thought and didn't say anything. I leaned forward and stared into his eyes, wanting him to know that if somehow I got free I'd kill him.

He got the message.

'OK, so you think you're a tough guy? Well, we'll soon find out!' he growled, then ordered the guards to lay me down on the floor, face up.

They pinned me down and I couldn't move.

He produced what looked like a pillow case and dunked it in the dustbin water. He also had a green plastic watering can that he filled up.

He knelt down next to me and put the wet cloth over my face. Breathing was not easy.

And then he started pouring water over my nose and mouth.

I tried turning my head to one side but the guards, grip was solid and I panicked. The sensation of drowning was such that I arched my back in a convulsion as if shocked by electricity. I fought against the restraint and the two big guards had to work hard to keep me down. I blew against the cloth that ballooned out a little and I got some air.

The interrogator stopped pouring water.

I lay there gasping. Trying to get enough breath.

'Number, rank and name,' he demanded.

I said nothing and the break in the torture was just long enough for me to recover sufficiently to start thinking.

'There must be a way to counter this,' I thought.

'They won't kill you. This is just an exercise.'

'Try and relax. Don't struggle. The more I struggle the more air I need.'

'I'll find the prick that's doing this and cut his balls off.'

That hate and the more rational thinking helped me greatly with the second dose. It was still frightening but I tried taking just shallow quick breaths through my mouth, then blowing hard with my nose followed by a quick nasal intake of air before the water arrived again.

The interrogator I think realised he had lost ground with me and I could hear frustrated muttering as he tightened the cloth over my face and filled up the watering can again.

The third dose started with a prolonged uninterrupted period of water being poured over my mouth and nose. I struggled to maintain the routine I'd used in the second dose and it didn't work. My brain started telling me this prick would go too far. It might just be an exercise but that wouldn't stop accidents happening.

He refilled the watering can and started again very quickly. I was still gasping as the water poured down again and this time he didn't stop. As the watering can emptied I couldn't breathe. I convulsed again and fought the guards.

Angry and frustrated my brain was shouting 'Eff you all!'

I was very close to breaking.

A voice said, 'That's enough. Take him away.'

Back at the pigsty I was starting to feel a bit sorry for myself. I was desperately tired, mentally shattered and physically damaged.

I was hungry but at least I wasn't thirsty any more. I managed a wry smile to myself. Right now, if I never saw water again that would be just fine with me.

I shuddered as a breeze blew into the pigsty. A robin sang from some bushes behind me. They usually sing in the early morning and early evening.

I suddenly perked up with the realization that my target of lasting for 36 hours was now very much within reach.

With all the water ingestion I suddenly needed a pee. I now understood why the crotch had been cut out of the shorts as the warm yellow liquid trickled down my leg, stinging the cuts on my ankles and feet.

The interrogators had another crack at me a couple of hours after dark. I stood under the bright spotlight and was bombarded with questions and insults. I ignored them and focussed on enjoying the warmth of the light bulb. I was by now quite happy. I'd not said a word for over 36 hours.

One of the interrogators came over to me. He was a short man, hairline well receded on the sides of his shining skull.

He pointed his finger at me. 'We're not worried. You'll talk in the morning, mark my words.'

He nearly caught me. I came so close to blurting out 'Eff you' but luckily my brain pulled the plug on my tongue in the nick of time. I'd been told that once you start talking that's the end, and this was just another way of challenging me to open my mouth.

It was a close call but it had a positive effect.

'I'll show you, dickhead! I'll keep quiet for another day,' I said to myself when back in the relative safety of my pigsty.

The night passed with regular water dousing and it was freezing cold, but they left me alone. Their priority would be on more recent captures that would have current information about the RV points. I could wait until morning.

I managed to doze a little while standing up. My body wanted a deep sleep, but every time I reached that point I'd stumble on my feet and wake up. I stood there shivering with my eyes closed. My feet and ankles hurt from the stone running, my back ached from the endless standing, my belly rumbled in discontent at having no food, and my head ached from the whole dammed business.

'Eff you all, but I won't talk for another day.'

The robin started singing and we received our final dousing of the night as the sun started to rise. An hour or two later the sun reached the pigsties and I had a rare few moments of pleasure as my body warmed up.

That day I was twice interrogated, thankfully without receiving any more of the water torture, and twice the guards took me for a run over the stones. The second time was late afternoon and it was during that run that I made the mistake that was to be my undoing.

As the guards turned me round at the top of the run for the return trip I opened my mouth for the first time.

From listening to conversations I'd worked out that after Umtali the exercise pipeline changed direction north towards the highlands of Inyanga where the SAS ran their selection courses. It made sense. They knew the country and a lot of it was unoccupied national parkland.

'I don't know how you pricks think I'm going to finish this exercise,' I said as my foot again crashed into a jagged rock. 'There's still at least a hundred kilometres to go and I won't be able to walk if you keep this up.'

'Tough shit!' one of them sneered and they increased the pace across the rocks.

I gritted my teeth and thought these would be another two who would lose their balls if I ever caught up with them afterwards.

The third night was a real struggle and in truth I was finished.

I kept falling asleep, only to be rudely woken as I lurched over, wrenching my arms in the process. My whole body ached. I couldn't stand anymore but managed to kneel on the cold rough concrete. The eagle owl called but I hardly noticed. The drenching by water made me shiver but I didn't care.

Human beings aren't made to be kept standing up without sleep for two days and three nights. I hadn't said a word under interrogation. I didn't care about that anymore either. For me this show was now over.

Thankfully I was spared humiliation.

There was a warm sun as I was led to the interrogation centre. Instead of being taken inside the darkened room I was sat down at a BBQ table outside on a small piece of lawn.

The short balding man who had said I'd talk yesterday approached and smiled. He put a cup of coffee on the table with a couple of ginger biscuits.

'Take off the handcuffs and leg irons,' he told the guards, which they did and then were dismissed.

'Mick, the coffee and biscuits are for you,' he said.

Without saying anything I dunked a biscuit into the hot coffee. It was the best biscuit I've ever had.

'Mick,' he said as I sipped the coffee, 'You have done well. We know you want to finish off the exercise so this evening you will be released at the current RV point. Have the other biscuit and some more coffee then for the records we'd like to hear what you did up until your capture.'

And it all came bubbling out. How I'd run along the railway to avoid tracking, finding the garage workshop, watching others get caught.

And then I stopped, suddenly realising what had happened.

The guards must have told him I'd spoken. How else would he know that I was worried about finishing the exercise? He had skilfully lulled me into a false sense of security and I'd started talking.

He realized at once that I had belatedly tumbled to the ploy.

'It's very true,' he said. 'As soon as you open your mouth that's the end. And I think I have just proven that to you.'

'Why didn't you talk and spare yourself yesterday?' he continued. 'You had done enough by then. You wouldn't have compromised anyone.'

'You said I'd talk in the morning. Mark my words,' I replied.

He nodded.

'And I said "Fuck you!"'

He laughed and left the table.

He returned a short while later with my clothes, a towel and a bar of soap.

'Get yourself cleaned up,' he said, 'then go to the medical room we have set up in the hall. They will do something for your feet and there are bunks there where you can rest. You will be back on the run tonight.'

Later that afternoon as I prepared to rejoin the exercise, one of the medics came in with a pair of socks.

'Here Mick,' he said, handing them over to me. 'Keep your boot laces loose, and with two pairs of socks you might just make it to Inyanga.'

As it got dark we were ushered onto a Land Rover with a canvas canopy open at the back. We were given a brown paper bag. I waited until last. The tailgate was secured behind me as I sat down.

The vehicle wound through the streets and began the steep climb up into the Christmas Pass hills that bordered the town.

About halfway up we were behind a big truck. It belched diesel smoke as it crawled upwards in the lowest of gears. There was a corner up ahead so the Land Rover couldn't pass. It was the chance I was waiting for.

I stood up, put a leg over the tailgate and found the tow bar. I heaved myself over, jumped onto the road and darted into the bushes.

There were partisans in this town that I knew would help me reach Inyanga intact.

I followed an animal track along the top of the bush-covered ridge line and kept going east. Eventually I reached a track junction I recognised. I turned right and started moving down the hill slopes towards street lights I could see in the distance.

An hour later I knocked on the front door.

A dog barked and the door opened.

'Hello Mum,' I said as Shep, our big black German Shepherd, jumped up at me.

In between mouthfuls of cold roast beef and hot coffee, generously laced with Cape brandy by my father, I told them of my ordeal. I finished by saying that I wanted to complete the exercise but was worried about the damage done to my ankles and feet, and the fact that the finishing line was still over one hundred kilometres away.

I took the sketch map out of the brown paper bag I'd been given while my father got out a road map. We found the RV that was about forty kilometres away.

'To give my feet a rest for another day, how about you driving me up to the RV in the morning?' I asked.

'We'll have to leave early, before the police and the SAS get on the road. I don't want to be caught by them again.'

'No problem. We'll leave at five,' said my father, who I could see was excited by the conspiracy.

Before getting some more much-needed sleep my parents helped me with a few items that would make the last stages of the exercise that much better for me. I firstly found an old backpack, and I added a blanket. It would be getting progressively higher and colder at night as I made my way towards Inyanga.

I took a plastic water bottle, food, and an old pair of Minolta binoculars so I could observe the RVs from well beyond the range of a dog's nose.

Next morning as we were driving towards Inyanga, my father told me about his escape and evasion experience.

He was co-pilot in a Lancaster bomber, part of a Pathfinder Squadron that had to locate and mark with incendiaries the targets for the main bombing wave that followed them.

It was March 1942, and he and Mum hadn't long been married.

Over the target the aircraft was badly hit by 'flak' – anti-aircraft gunfire. One of the two starboard engines took a big hit and stopped. Shell fragments peppered the aircraft and did structural damage, but everyone was OK and the plane was still flying.

They were over France with the English Channel in sight when they were spotted by German escort fighters on their way back to base. Both gunners at the back of the aircraft were killed in the attack that followed, and the big bomber was mortally wounded. With flames and smoke coming from the plane, the captain, a Canadian called Jack Regan, ordered abandon ship.

They made their way out of the cockpit and opened the aircraft door.

'Captain goes last,' said Jack, and Dad jumped from the plane.

With his parachute open my father looked back at the plane. He got a fleeting glimpse of Jack who had hesitated at the door, and then the plane exploded.

He paused in his storytelling, struggling with emotion as he relived the horror.

He dug into a pocket, pulled out a small round badge and gave it to me.

There was the outline of a parachute against a gilt background, and beneath the word 'Caterpillar'.

Dad explained that all airmen who saved their lives by using a parachute during the war years automatically became members of the Caterpillar Club, the connection being the silk thread that parachutes were made from in those days.

He said he knew they were not far from the coast when they were shot down so he kept close to the hedgerows for cover and went in that direction. He passed a field of turnips and dug up two for food, then he stopped in cover of woodland and waited until it got dark.

He told me how he walked for most of the night, avoiding farm buildings and a village. He said it was cold and wet, and the flying boots he was wearing started to hurt his feet.

Half way through the second day his feet were hurting so much he decided to get help. He saw a small farm cottage and approached. He knocked on the door and was met by an elderly man and his wife. He couldn't speak French and they couldn't speak English but somehow he got across the message that his feet were very sore.

They helped him take off his boots and the woman got a bowl of warm water and bathed his blistered feet. While this was happening, the man said something and left the house.

He returned some time later accompanied by a German infantry patrol. My father was captured because he'd unwittingly sought assistance from a couple who were pro-German Vichy French.

'What troubled me most,' he said, 'was that I knew I would be reported as missing. Joan (my mother) would be notified but she wouldn't know if I was alive or dead, and I had no way of getting a message to her. I couldn't bear the thought of her anxiety, and there was nothing I could do about it.

'Seven months later the Red Cross came to our prison camp and they eventually got a message back to her. She said later that she'd never given up hoping I was alive.

'I didn't see her for two and a half years.'

I sat in silence for a while, trying to imagine what it was like for both of them.

'Listening to your story makes me feel pretty bad about getting a ride like this,' I said.

'No!' he replied at once. 'Riding your luck and taking your chances is all part of the game. You were unlucky to be caught because of the dog, but in jumping off the back of that Land Rover you were making your own luck. The same happened with me towards the end of the war.

'I'll tell you about that next time you are home. I think this is the RV up ahead,' he added.

I watched as the white Zephyr Zodiac disappeared back down the road, then I headed off towards some bush-covered high ground where I'd spend the day, resting and watching with my binoculars.

With the state of my feet I couldn't rush in at the last minute, grab the bag then run off as fast as I could, so I closed in gradually, dropped my pack and binoculars, and made the RV without incident.

'Two legs to go,' I was told.

I walked through the night and with two pairs of socks and loose laces it wasn't too bad.

As the sky began to lighten I found a dense thicket of low bushes and bracken fern. I crawled into the middle and curled up in my blanket.

It was still some distance to the next RV and I wasn't moving fast, so I set out again in the middle of the day. In front of me was a large expanse of grassland and heather. I'd seen a helicopter earlier in the morning so trying to cross in broad daylight would be madness, and I had no wish for a repeat of stone running or water treatment.

My only safe option was to go around the open ground. It would be a lot longer but there was a wattle plantation that would keep me in cover.

It turned out to be a good option. I found a rough track that had been cut between the trees. There were old tractor tyre tracks but clearly it was seldom used, and if I heard or saw anything coming it would be easy to disappear into the thick forest on either side.

I made good progress.

As the afternoon passed I heard the noise of machinery in front of me, and as I got closer I could see plumes of white steam or smoke above the tree line. It was the factory that extracted tannin from the wattle bark.

I detoured around the open site and looked back at it with my binoculars from a high vantage point. There was a camouflaged Land Rover parked next to a building.

It had a canvas canopy over the back, like the one I had jumped from on Christmas Pass.

I changed my position slightly and there sitting in the sun with a beer in his hand was our mortar platoon sergeant. There were another two sergeants and a corporal also enjoying the sun and a beer.

The three sergeants had all been with me in the back of the train at the start of the exercise. The corporal was also from the mortar platoon and they used these covered vehicles instead of the open Sabres used by the troops.

I realised exactly what was going on. This was the power of the NCOs mess at work.

The sergeants would have obtained details of the exercise from sergeants working with our Training Troop. After being dropped off my guess was they had arranged to be picked up by the corporal and driven to this factory where obviously they knew someone who would look after them until the exercise finale. On the last day they would triumphantly arrive at the finishing line with big smiles and a cock and bull story about how they were too clever to be caught.

'You bloody wankers!' I thought. 'This attitude is exactly what the Brigadier was trying to get out of the unit, and you pricks are giving him two fingers up.'

And every time I jarred my ankles as I approached the last RV point, the more it pissed me off.

As usual I waited until the last minute before heading towards the RV and my last brown paper bag of the exercise. The coast looked clear and I closed in.

Ken Philipson was there. He asked me how I was getting on.

'As a matter of fact Ken, right now I'm feeling really pissed off,' I replied, then went on to tell him what I'd seen earlier in the afternoon.

'Thanks, Mick,' he said. 'None of them have been to a single RV so we suspected something was going on. The Brigadier will not be happy about this.'

I thanked him and headed back into cover. I had twenty-five kilometres to go to reach the finish line.

'You ride your luck,' my father had said. 'Yes,' I thought, 'but you don't push your luck!'

A great guy from the Brit Paras called Pete Cole took over the mortar platoon not long after the exercise and we were to use them with huge success on many future missions.

At the end we were all given new clothes and told to shave and clean up. We were then taken to the Rhodes Inyanga Hotel where a big table had been laid and the bar was open.

The Brigadier called for our attention and started by warning us to take it slow with the beer. We'd been starved and on the run for two weeks. Best to take it easy.

He thanked us all for participating in the exercise and for taking it as seriously as we did. He said we had all done well and that would be noted on our confidential reports at the year end.

I noticed he had sensibly excluded the interrogators and the Military Police from the gathering. After a couple of beers some us would be thinking about getting even.

Before sitting down to big T-bone steaks, the Brigadier circulated to speak to us all individually.

'Great head butt, Mick,' he said with a smile as he reached me.

'Thank you, Sir,' I replied. 'Just a pity I couldn't do more damage. Who was he out of interest?' I asked.

'Special Branch Police from Bulawayo and I don't think he'll forget this exercise in a hurry. You weren't the only one to give him trouble. It was a good lesson for them too. They are obviously not used to dealing with people who fight back and some of you put up a spirited resistance.'

'I was thinking about it afterwards, Sir,' I replied, 'and I don't think it was too clever. If I did that to a Zambian Police interrogator you can only imagine what would have happened to me. Have you got plenty of those pills you showed us at the start?' I asked.

'Enough to go round,' he said over his shoulder as he turned to the airman standing next to me.

In the next couple of years, I carried a pill on three or four occasions.

Thankfully they were never needed and were phased out as we perfected our skills in the art of bush warfare.

Getting the Boot

Detective Inspector Phil Roberts was an English-trained policeman working a five-year contract with the Rhodesian Police. Phil had good experience with the CID in England and it was decided to put him with the counter-terrorism desk of Special Branch in Salisbury.

He'd been there a little over three years and was doing well. He'd notched up a couple of good successes, he was an easygoing character with a good sense of humour, and was well liked by his work colleagues.

In December 1968 Phil was tasked with finding an African police recruit who was willing to join one of the terrorist groups operating against the country. The idea was he would be trained by them and then once deployed back in the country he would desert and bring the accrued information on training, bases and personnel back to Special Branch.

Phil studied the background and course results of the recruits currently undergoing training and picked out Henry Munyaradzi. Henry came from Fort Victoria in the south eastern part of the country that so far was untouched by terrorism or nationalistic demonstrations. It meant he would have no background or profile that could arouse suspicion with the terrorist groups, and it was felt they would probably welcome recruits from areas yet to be infiltrated by their gangs.

Phil arranged a private meeting with Henry and explained what he wanted. He said that for as long as Henry was away the Police would pay his wages into a bank, and on his return they would give him a bonus payment of $5,000 and employ him as a Police Constable.

Phil said it was vital for his safety that he told nobody about this discussion. He told him to think about it overnight, and then he wanted a decision.

Next morning Henry Munyaradzi decided to become a ZANU terrorist.

In the two days that followed, Phil Roberts prepared Henry for his mission. He was given some second-hand clothes and a pair of Chinese made boots that would have belonged to a former terrorist. They were new looking and Henry found them comfortable. The moulded thick rubber sole had a distinctive figure 8 tread that was well known to security forces.

On the inside of the boot, sewn into the lower part of the tongue, Phil had put a small laundry label with his name. This would never be seen by anyone but when Henry chose to defect from his terrorist group, he could show it to the security forces or police who could then authenticate his identity as an undercover policeman run by Phil Roberts.

Henry was given some money and told to take the bus to the small settlement of Rusambo in the Rushinga district, close to the border with Mozambique in the north east of the country.

Special Branch knew that several villages on both sides of the border were sympathetic towards ZANU and helped with the passage of recruits through Mozambique and into Zambia where political indoctrination and basic military training began.

Henry later told of how he'd bought some items in the small store at Rusambo and in the course of conversation had let it be known he was going to join the fighters. It wasn't long before he was directed to a village where he stayed for three days. In appreciation he gave the headman's wife what money he had left to pay for his food.

On the third day three ZANU fighters arrived and took him and five others staying in neighbouring villages away for training. They walked through Mozambique staying in the bush and avoiding roads. His comrades told him they were quite safe because the Portuguese stayed on the roads and in their bases and never ventured into the bush.

It took them over a week to reach the shores of Lake Cahora Basa. They rested for two days at a fishing village and then crossed to the north bank in dugout canoes. From there they headed west to the Zambian border, crossing the Luangwa River and eventually reaching the small settlement of Kapoche where ZANU had a truck.

From Kapoche they drove to 'Freedom Camp' not far north of Lusaka on the road to Ndola, where for the first time Henry realised the extent of the organisation and what he was getting himself into.

Freedom Camp housed over seven hundred ZANU personnel, most of them recruits undergoing training. Henry described how dignitaries such as Herbert Chitepo and Josiah Tongogara came to the camp to address the recruits and urge them on in what they called 'The Great War of Chimurenga'.

One day he was surprised when a Chinese soldier spoke to them about Mao Tse Tung and how he was changing the world. They were all given copies of Mao's *Little Red Book* which the Chinese man said had replaced the Bible.

Henry stayed at Freedom Camp for eight months before being chosen for advanced training at a camp in Tanzania.

A convoy of four trucks took one hundred ZANU recruits north-east to the narrow border that ran between Lake Tanganyika to the north and Lake Nyasa to the south. After crossing into Tanzania, they passed through the town of Mbeya and on to the settlement of Iringa, not far from the famous Morogoro Crater Game Reserve.

Close to Iringa the Chinese had built a training camp for the Mozambique Frelimo terrorist group. It was known as Mugagao.

The camp had been operational for a few years when the Chinese urged Frelimo to invite ZANU cadres to join them for training. ZANU and Frelimo became close allies as a result and they later fought together against the Rhodesian security forces and the Renamo rebel group in Mozambique.

Henry was once again overawed by the scale of everything. As a police recruit, he knew of these terrorist organisations, but never imagined them to be so well supported with people and equipment. Container loads of weapons, mines, grenades, explosives and clothing from China were delivered on the railway the Chinese had built between Dar es Salaam and Lusaka. How could anything like this be stopped he wondered?

With discipline already instilled through his police training, Henry's commitment to his training at Freedom Camp and Mugagao came naturally. It was noticed and he was picked out for further instruction. They wanted Henry to become a trainer.

He spent a year at Mugagao then was moved back to Freedom Camp to take up a training role. He'd been there for two months when he and five others were called into a meeting. They had been selected to infiltrate into the Karoi area of Rhodesia where with assistance from local tribes they would wage a short hit-and-run campaign against the white farming community.

It was explained that these were the tactics taught by Mao Tse Tung.

They would spring surprise attacks and lay mines in the roads, then move quickly away from the area and back into Zambia before the security forces could react.

With the security forces' attention focussed on the attack area they would then create confusion by striking in a completely different location, far removed from the initial attack. That group would again disappear back into the bush before the security forces could respond.

They would slowly intensify these hit-and-run raids that would force the enemy to spread their resources far and wide, and create fear and uncertainty through the rural communities.

One night in January 1971 Henry's group crossed the Zambezi River on the eastern side of the Mana Pools Game Reserve, landing on a broad sandspit that marked the confluence of the Sapi River that flowed down from the escarpment hills forty kilometres away. They would follow the river up into the hills and on towards their target area.

It was the rainy season. Water would not be a problem, and they were hoping the rain would wash away their tracks.

Being tracked and killed by security forces was Henry's biggest fear.

He spoke to the others in his gang about it, and took off a boot to show them the distinct figure 8 track that he said was well known to security forces. Better, he suggested, to go barefoot at the start and use boots only once they reached the hard, stony ground of the escarpment hills.

If their barefoot tracks were found by game rangers or security forces there would be no suggestion in the prints that they were terrorists. The tracks could well be dismissed as those of local hunters or poachers.

Nobody disagreed and they all packed away their boots.

The canoes dropped them off on the sandbank and returned to Zambia.

They were now on their own on a dangerous mission but they were excited about it.

Henry stayed at the back of the group, and as they began to move away from the river, he took the boot with the name sewn into the tongue from his pack and deliberately dropped it on the sandbank.

It was a message.

They marched off into the night.

In the Zambezi Valley bigger rivers like the Sapi had their origins deep in the escarpment hills, and in that broken rocky country there were permanent water holes. In the hot dry season, the game animals – elephant, buffalo, zebra and all the big antelope – moved into the hills to reach the water and as a result wide game tracks were formed.

The gang followed one of these well-used game tracks that led them towards the distant hills. The going was easy underfoot and there was every chance a herd of elephant or buffalo would later obscure their barefoot tracks.

The following night on the pretext of taking a toilet stop, Henry deserted the gang.

For the next two and a half days he followed the edge of the escarpment hills heading west because he knew he would eventually reach the main road leading to the border post at Chirundu. He would flag down a car and ask to be taken to the nearest police station.

Henry eventually reached the road. He took the magazine off the AK47 he was carrying and squeezed the weapon into his pack. The end of the gun barrel protruded slightly but there was nothing more he could do except put the pack out of sight behind a tree. He sat in the shade and waited for a vehicle to arrive.

After about half an hour he heard an engine noise. He stood up and went to the side of the road. It was a camouflaged army Land Rover. He waved energetically at it and the vehicle came to a halt next to him.

A soldier carrying a rifle got out and in passable Shona asked him who he was and what was the problem.

'I am a policeman,' Henry replied in English.

'It is important I get to a police station as quickly as possible. There is a terrorist group I have to report.'

The young soldier was suspicious. Henry looked like a terrorist but his claim to be a policeman was confusing.

Sensing his hesitation Henry told him to go behind the nearby tree and there he would find his pack.

The driver, a sergeant, had by now got out of the vehicle and was pointing his SLR rifle at Henry.

The soldier went behind the tree and found the pack.

'Holy Christ Sarge! This guy's a gook!' he cried out as he saw the AK muzzle protruding from the pack.

The sergeant came up into the aim with his rifle.

Henry put up his hands. 'I am a policeman,' he said again.

'This can be explained. Please take me to the police station.'

The sergeant was confused. Why would a real gook want to go to a police station?

'Tie him up and put him in the back, and you sit next to him with your rifle pointed at his head. If there is any hint of funny business pull the trigger,' he ordered.

Henry sat as still as he could, not daring to move, fearful of getting shot when he was now so close to getting back to civilisation and collecting his reward.

They drove up the winding road that traversed the escarpment hills and eventually reached the small settlement of Makuti. There was a hotel, a store with fuel pumps and a police station. They took Henry inside and called the Member-in-Charge, Inspector Bill Lendrum.

'We've picked up a gook who claims to be a policeman,' said the sergeant. 'He asked to be taken to the nearest police station because he had to report a terrorist group that has come into the country.'

'Where is this terrorist group?' the inspector asked immediately.

'On the Sapi River heading for Karoi. There are five of them – ZANU fighters. They will be well into the hills by now,' Henry replied.

'And you say you are a policeman?' he asked.

'Yes, Sir. My name is Henry Munyaradzi. I was a police cadet under training in Salisbury when I was approached by a Special Branch officer called Phil Roberts. He wanted me to join the terrorist organisation so I could report on their bases and operations.

'That was in December 1968. I have been away at training camps in Zambia and Tanzania since then. This is my first mission and the only chance I have had of leaving the terrorist organisation.'

'Thank you, Henry,' said the inspector. 'I'll check on that, but meanwhile I'm going to put you in a cell while we take action on your report.'

Bill Lendrum alerted the police at Karoi. A troop of Rhodesian Light Infantry commandos were camped nearby and were soon on the hunt for the remaining five terrorists.

He then called Special Branch headquarters in Salisbury and asked for Pete Stanton. He and Pete had been on the same course at police college. Bill made a career with uniform branch while Pete branched off into the intelligence world with Special Branch.

He explained the situation.

'What concerns me most about this is that I've never heard of a Phil Roberts, and my worry is this could be some kind of ZANU trick. I've checked his pack and can't see anything in the way of explosives that could threaten us. But I'm not taking chances, so until we have concrete proof that this was indeed a police recruit used by Special Branch he will stay in the cells.'

'Yes, I agree,' replied Pete. 'The name rings a bell but there is no Phil Roberts in Special Branch at the moment. I'll check personnel records and payroll to see what I can come up with. I'll call you back later then I'm going to drive up to speak to the man. One way or the other he should have some interesting stuff to tell us.'

Pete Stanton called less than an hour later.

There was a Phil Roberts who used to work on the counter-terrorism desk of Special Branch, but he had left the police a year ago and only Ricky May, supreme head of Special Branch would have been aware of any such recruitment. Unfortunately the boss was away on long overseas leave and was not immediately contactable.

Personnel did have a record of Henry Munyaradzi as a cadet in 1968 but he did not complete the training course, however for some reason he had been paid weekly ever since. Checking with the bank there had been no transactions on the account since it was opened in 1968.

Pete explained that while it looked likely he was an undercover policeman, Henry Munyaradzi should stay in the cells for further questioning.

Pete Stanton met Henry the following afternoon and started the interrogation.

Henry described in detail what happened at the start and how he was eventually picked up by ZANU in a village near Rusambo.

'Before we get into the detail about ZANU is there anything you have that can prove you were recruited by Phil Roberts?' Pete asked. Adding that it was a standard operating procedure to give plants something that would prove their true identity.

Henry thought about it for a moment or two and then he remembered.

'My boots,' he said with enthusiasm.

'Phil gave me a pair of Chinese issue boots and on the tongue on the inside of the boot he had sewn a label with his name.'

'That's good,' said Pete. 'Let's go and have a look'.

Henry's face dropped.

'I'm sorry. We can't, and he went on to explain how he had left the boot with the label on a sandbank after they crossed from Zambia. He'd done it in the hope that game rangers or security forces would find it, see the label and let Phil know he was back in the country.

'We need to get that boot,' said Pete as he left the cell and went to find a telephone.

The Brigadier took the call and agreed at once.

In the SAS we didn't have Military Police – we didn't need them – but somebody had to look after the barracks when the administrative and training teams that worked there during the day had gone home. We ran a duty officer system, with rostered duty signallers, and used recruits or troops back in town for training or stand-by duties as camp guards.

I was back in town on ten days R and R. I had an overseas trip planned to visit my grandfather who lived at Morecombe Bay in Lancashire, and I was trying to save money.

No better way of keeping out of the bars and restaurants than volunteering to be duty officer, and it wasn't bad at all. I spent the days working out in the gym, relaxing at the swimming pool, and sometimes I'd take a Sabre Land Rover with a VHF radio and go birdwatching in one of the nearby woodland areas.

I'd just finished dinner in the Officers' Mess when Jimmy Munro, our Signals Officer walked into the dining room.

'Mick,' he said, 'the Brigadier wants you to call him urgently.'

I jumped up and went with him to our operations room where I made the call.

The Brigadier explained the situation with the terrorist claiming to be a police plant at Makuti.

'It's important for Special Branch and the long-term security of this individual, especially if he does turn out to be a police plant, for as few people as possible to know about this. That's why Pete Stanton has asked the SAS to get involved to recover his boot. Special Branch trust us and our discretion.

'So, I want you to lead a team with another four – whoever you can find in the barracks at the moment – to go to the Sapi River in the morning and see if you can find it. You will parachute into the area and I will organise a helicopter recovery once you have either found the boot, or when you believe there is nothing more you can do.

'I have already been in contact with the air force. They want you at the parachute school no later than 0400 for a first-light drop next to the river. Mick, I hope to have you out and back home tomorrow night, but you know how things can pan out so make sure you'll be OK for at least three days.'

I acknowledged everything and put the phone down.

'Jimmy, I'm going to need your help,' I said to our signals officer, and went on to explain the mission I had just been given.

I needed Jimmy firstly to stand in for me as duty officer, and secondly, I asked if he'd let his duty signals operator come with me as part of the team.

Ralph Moore was ex Brit Paras and as you'd expect from that regiment a dammed good soldier. But 'Ralph the Rat', as we called him because of his short stature, was also an outstanding all-round signaller and an exceptional Morse code operator, and we'd need such skills to get comms through from such a remote area.

Jimmy agreed at once and at the same time said he and Ralph would sort out all the radios and code books we'd need while I tried to find another three SAS men and get everything else organised.

My first stop was the Sergeants' Mess. Here I found Kevin Cook who was duty NCO, and I told him my story.

'Count me in, Mick,' he said. 'This place will survive without a duty sergeant for a couple of days.'

I couldn't have been happier. Kevin was easygoing and humorous, but he was also a very good operator and had done well in action.

He suggested we go up to the main barracks to see who, if anyone, was at home.

We found two men watching TV in the canteen.

'Sorry boys, but we are about to spoil your evening,' Kevin said, and went on to tell them they would be joining us in a hunt for an old boot.

'If Mick wasn't with you, I'd have said you'd been drinking, Sarge,' said lanky Billy Grant with a smile on his face.

'Mick, I hope we will be rewarded at the end of this?' asked Ginger Thompson, his companion. 'The Order of the Boot will look bloody good next to my general service medal.'

I laughed along with them. This was certainly unusual but we'd done some weird things before and I was sure this wouldn't be the last.

The following morning, we had a look at the maps with the DC3 pilots and picked an open flood plain as our drop zone. Both Kevin and

I knew the place. There were low anthill mounds with stunted mlala palms but no other trees to speak of. It would be a good DZ for us and only about a kilometre away from the Sapi River.

The pilots took the aircraft up to 1,000 feet, our drop height, and maintained it all the way to the Zambezi Valley. Once over the escarpment Trevor Smith, the despatcher, gave us the order to stand up and hook up.

We hooked up our packs to the quick release device and attached the big static line hook to the overhead cable while Trevor checked everything. He bunched us together close to the exit door as the aircraft closed in on our DZ.

Red light. 'Stand in the door!' yelled Trevor.

We shuffled forward and I steadied myself by holding the door frame with my right hand. Left arm out of the way, folded on top of the reserve chute.

Green light. 'Go! Go! Go! Go! Go!' shouted Trevor as the five of us stumbled past him and leapt into space.

The big brown T10 chutes opened cleanly and we drifted down in perfect conditions.

I had a quick look round then flicked the quick release device. My pack dropped away and dangled beneath me on the three-metre rope.

There was very little wind but I had some forward momentum so pulled down on the back-rigging lines to slow my descent. My pack landed first as I angled my ankles for a forward right landing. The ground was hard but the descent was slow so landing was OK.

I collapsed the canopy by pulling on one of the shoulder Capewell releases and before getting out of the harness, unstrapped my FN rifle, took it out of the canvas sleeve, attached a magazine and cocked. I knelt down next to my pack and had a good look round. We were after all on a known terrorist incursion route.

I looked behind me. The others were all close and they too were ready for action.

After a couple of minutes, I guessed it was all clear so stood up to get out of the parachute harness. The others followed suit.

We bundled up the parachute equipment and our helmets and left them in an open space where they would easily be seen by the helicopter crew that would come in later to recover everything.

I pulled out the maps and we all had a good look.

The big game trail, that we knew followed the river up into the hills, was on the opposite side of the Sapi to us, so I suggested we cross and pick it up, hoping we might also find the tracks of the terrorist group.

The Sapi had big pools where there were bends in the river but between them the water flowed in shallow braided streams across the sandy bed. A small herd of buffalo were at one of the bigger pools about four hundred metres away from us. I was happy they were too busy at the water to notice us.

We picked up the track and had a close look at the ground. No sign of human footprints, just the recent hoof marks of the buffalo, overlaying the wider prints of elephant.

We headed downstream towards the river mouth.

We'd been walking for about twenty minutes when suddenly Billy Grant who was at the back of our file shouted out.

We stopped in alarm, swivelling round, rifles at the ready.

There, no more than five metres away from Billy, was a lioness. She'd stopped when he turned around and backed off a couple more paces when the rest of us came alongside him, but she didn't go away.

We all soon realised this was a lioness on her way to the happy hunting grounds.

The wretched animal was skin and bone, her coat was tight over rippled rib bones, and there were bare patches of pink skin on her back. Deep within hollow sockets her eyes streamed and I was sure she was blind.

I didn't want to fire a shot, although that would have been the humane thing to do, but I couldn't have her trying to make Billy Grant her last supper.

While she stood there blankly staring in our direction, I had an idea.

I told the boys to watch her while I dug into my pack.

I took out a tin of bully beef, twisted the small handle to open it and nudged the lump of meat into my hand.

I broke it into two lumps then went forward towards the lioness and lobbed half of it on the ground in front of her nose.

She didn't move while I did this and I was again sure she was blind, but I reasoned that her nose would still be good so she should smell the bully beef.

The lioness lifted her head a couple of times and we could see she was sniffing the air. She put her head down and followed her nose until she found the meat. She picked it up and gulped it down.

I lobbed the second half of the meat off to one side. I knew she would smell it and eventually find it, but it would take time, and by then we would be gone.

We moved on down the track, Billy nervously checking behind him as we went, but we didn't see the lioness again.

As we approached the Zambezi River, we moved into cover to watch and listen.

I scanned the opposite bank with my binoculars, looking for movement or any sign of recent human activity. After half an hour I was confident we were on our own, so we stood up and made our way to the long sand bank created by the convergence of the Sapi.

And there it was.

A boot.

Standing upright on top of the sand one hundred metres in front of us.

I picked it up and spread apart the laces so I could see inside.

There, on a dirty stained label in red embroidery cotton was the name 'P. Roberts'.

We retreated back into cover away from the river and I asked Ralph to set up the HF radio.

Twenty minutes later the Brigadier received the Morse code message, and an hour after that we heard a helicopter heading our way.

As we lifted off, I pointed out the location of our parachutes that they would collect later.

The helicopter climbed to clear the escarpment hills and headed for Makuti, where the boot was given to Pete Stanton. Before heading off to the air base at Lake Kariba, Henry Munyaradzi and Pete came out to see us as he wanted to thank us for getting the boot – his ticket back to normal life.

As I shook his hand I said, 'Thank you for what you have done, Henry. You are a very brave man.'

We were shuttled back to Kariba, the helicopter left to recover our parachutes, and by late afternoon we had them with us in an air force Britten-Norman Islander on our way home.

The five of us had a few beers, a good dinner and an early night and that should have been the end of the story.

But it wasn't.

How often have we all said 'It's a small world these days'?

My wife and I were browsing through Selfridges store in London while on overseas leave, and on turning around the end of an aisle bumped into our neighbours from New Zealand.

On another occasion I was waiting to be served at a chemist shop in Zurich when there was a tap on my shoulder. It was the sales manager from a security company I knew based in the small town of Marten in the North Island.

More than twenty years later my wife Sharen and I were visiting my aging parents who had chosen to stay on living in Harare, the new capital of Zimbabwe. They told us of how local African soapstone sculptors had formed a co-operative and bought a piece of land at a place known as 'Balancing Rocks'. They said the co-op members had built a garden around these natural granite wonders where they displayed their works. It was a huge success and had attracted customers from all over the world keen to own some of this unique art work.

One afternoon we went to see for ourselves.

We were immediately impressed by the natural setting. There were red flowering aloes branching out from clusters of grey granite boulders, each the size of a car, some balancing at crazy angles and extensions. I looked to see if it was artificial with steel or concrete supports, but it was all natural.

Brightly coloured sunbirds darted between the aloe flowers, while in the shade trees yellow weaver birds had built nests that dangled down from the outer branches.

And scattered on the ground between the rock clusters was the art work.

Many of the half human and half animal forms did not appeal to us aesthetically, but there were some stunning works, and all without exception were very skilfully carved from big lumps of beautiful soapstone.

Some of the creations were very big and would weigh in excess of a ton. Some of the carvings were all polished; the deep green and browns of the stone glistened in the sun. Others had selected parts cut and polished that contrasted with the dull natural outer texture of the stone.

It was a magnificent exhibition and we were totally engrossed in it.

As we walked through the garden, we noticed the art was organised into patches; each patch the work of an individual artist. We read about each artist as we progressed in the catalogue we had been given.

I stopped suddenly in front of a magnificent piece. A curled-up sleeping antelope made from deep green stone that had been highly polished. It was absolutely stunning.

Sharen took my hand. 'That is amazing,' she said, 'I know it's impossible but imagine that in our front garden at home.'

I agreed but what was even more amazing to me was the name of the sculptor.

On a low post on the ground was a sign saying this was the work of Henry Munyaradzi.

We progressed through the garden and ended up at a large thatched shelter with tables where smaller works were displayed for sale. A group of African men sat at one end of the shed and I guessed they were the artists.

One of them came close and I asked him if I could speak to Henry Munyaradzi. He went to find him for us.

A few minutes later a man of my height, clean shaven and carrying more weight than was good for him, approached and introduced himself as Henry.

I didn't recognise him at all, which was hardly surprising, but asked if we could talk privately outside.

We wandered off and perched together on one of the low balancing rocks.

'Henry,' I said, 'I once met a man with your name. He was an undercover policeman but there was uncertainty about his identity. I was sent to the Zambezi to find a boot that had a name sewn into the tongue – the name of the police officer who recruited him. We found the boot and all ended well. Before we flew off, he came to thank us for finding the boot…'

'And you said I was a very brave man,' interrupted Henry with a big smile on his face.

'What is your name?' he asked.

I introduced Sharen and then myself, explaining that at the time I was in the SAS but now we lived in New Zealand.

'Henry, it was a very courageous thing you did, but one for which you could never receive public recognition. I'm happy the secret is still intact. I have spoken to nobody about it – not even to Sharen. We must still keep the secret for as long as you are in Zimbabwe.'

'Thank you,' he said. 'It was a long time ago now so I believe I am safe, but yes, it is important we keep the secret.'

Henry went on to explain that he was given the promised reward, and that plus his accumulated unspent wages put him in a good position financially. He decided not to go back to the police, but instead chose to join his brother who had started carving soapstone near the great Zimbabwe Ruins.

He found he had an aptitude for carving and both he and his brother joined the co-operative of sculptors. With his money they were able to help set up the garden and exhibition centre.

'I cannot let you leave without taking a piece of my soapstone work with you,' he said at the end.

We thanked him and explained that while we would love to have one of his works they were too big and too heavy to ship to New Zealand.

'Come with me,' he said, and led us back into the hall and to one of the tables where a selection of smaller works was on display.

He picked out the head of an African woman and gave it to Sharen.

'This is Marina,' he said. 'Please take her to New Zealand. This is another secret that will be best off well away from Africa. I met Marina at the training camp at Mugagao in Tanzania. We fell in love, but I was an undercover policeman, and she was a ZANU terrorist. It broke our hearts when I was sent away, but it could never have worked.'

Marina sits on our dining table to this day.

She is carved from deep black soapstone. Her hair is thick and woolly, her lips pout invitingly, and she has high cheek bones that project pride and a degree of authority.

Marina is our treasure.

Henry and Marina are our secrets.

The Ghosts of Angola

In some circles the SAS are referred to as 'Army Troops'. It's a fair description because while we could be attached to divisions or brigades, we were not part of any divisional or brigade organisation and were never tasked by them.

We were an independent organisation, and largely self-sufficient, only needing help from others, such as the air force for example, who often were pivotal in our deployment or recovery, and who could keep us going with resupply.

We came under the control of the 'OCC' – the Operations Coordinating Committee – a joint services body led by the overall defence forces chief – an army general, the head of the air force, the police commissioner, and the head of the CIO – the Central Intelligence Organisation.

Anybody from any of the services could request SAS assistance, but all requests went to 'ComOps' for consideration by the OCC. This protocol also extended to the SAS itself, so if we had a particular operation in mind, we too had to get OCC approval before proceeding.

It was a good system, especially since General Peter Walls, the grand commander, was an SAS man. He had commanded the first C Squadron in Malaysia, he kept abreast of developments within the unit, and even came out now and then to do a parachute jump with us.

So there were no issues with our tasking. General Walls knew what we could do and he knew what was an SAS job and what was not.

The OCC, being at the top of the services tree, also worked with the senior echelons in government. Politicians from all walks of life who became ministers, would sometimes be called on by the OCC to look at the political implications of a proposed action.

Sometimes they – like everyone else – would approach the OCC requesting SAS assistance with something on their political agenda. The SAS were thus also known as 'Political Troops' and it was one such request from the Rhodesian Foreign Minister that led to our first deployment into Angola.

It was 1969 and the Cold War was still in full swing.

In Europe the Berlin Wall separated armoured divisions from East and West. Nuclear-armed American B-52 bombers patrolled the edge of Russian air space, while Tupolev Tu-95 'Bears' did the same off the Scottish coast.

Polaris and Russian Borei submarines, all armed with multiple nuclear warheads, were the ultimate guarantee in the concept of 'Mutually Assured Destruction'. With nuclear-armed submarines both sides had the ability to launch retaliatory attacks against the other nation in the event of a first strike.

In Asia the war raged in Vietnam.

Big numbers of Americans were being killed and humiliated in a war they didn't know how to fight. Bigger numbers of Vietcong were killed, and even bigger numbers of ordinary Vietnamese people were slaughtered either by getting caught up in the military action, or shockingly because they didn't conform with the communist image of a 'revolutionary'. Anyone with education for example, was a dead duck in Vietnam and they executed thousands of their own kind for this sort of reason.

In neighbouring China Mao Tse Tung was also killing his own people, on an even grander scale, in the so called 'cultural revolution'.

In Africa we didn't face any nuclear threat but the black power movements across the continent were supported by the Russians and the Chinese, and were not slow to adopt the communist ideology of brutal subjugation of the local population.

In our patch for example, Frelimo systematically killed off every traditional African chief as they advanced through the Niassa and Cabo Delgado provinces of northern Mozambique.

Both the Russians and the Chinese were intent on filling the power vacuum left by the British as the colonial empire they had created in Africa was abandoned, and in the process the communist bloc would get their hands on the amazing mineral wealth of the continent.

Both parties spread their influence by training and arming dissident groups.

In Zimbabwe for example, the Chinese backed Mugabe, his ZANU terrorist organisation and the majority Mashona tribe they represented, while the Russians supported the rival Matabele tribe led by Joshua Nkomo and his ZAPU terrorist group.

It developed into a race we called 'The Second Scramble for Africa'.

But regardless of the rivalry between factions, the undisputable fact was that in one form or another communist inspired insurrection was spreading like wildfire across Africa.

From their strongholds in the centre and south, the Portuguese, the Rhodesians and the South Africans were not prepared to just let this happen, but they were very different countries and cultures, with very different views on their positions in Africa.

The Portuguese had grand designs.

In Mozambique and Angola they saw the potential to create another Brazil, that with oil in the Cabinda province of Angola and all the other minerals would be even richer than their South American creation.

For the Rhodesians, it was all about independence and survival. They would not allow marauding communists to take over a prosperous country that was drifting towards multi-culturalism – at least until Smith and his Rhodesian Front extremists took over. The spread of communism gave them their *raison d'être.*

The South Africans had their own agenda.

Escaping religious persecution in Europe their early settlers established themselves in the Cape over 300 years ago, joining the slaves from Malaysia taken there by the Portuguese to service the transit base they established for their caravels sailing between Europe and Asia.

The early South Africans were forced out of the Cape by the British and trekked north into land occupied by African tribes. There were skirmishes with these African tribes and ultimately a disastrous conflict with the British in the Anglo Boer War.

There was also conflict between the Rhodesians and South Africans.

In 1897, responding to Boer control of the gold fields and the greed of people like Cecil Rhodes, the foolhardy Dr Leander Starr Jameson led a train-mounted raid with 400 men into the northern Transvaal. His entire force limply surrendered to the South Africans.

Many Rhodesians fought in the Anglo Boer War against South Africa, and later many South Africans were on the opposite side to the Rhodesians by favouring the Germans in the two world wars.

By the time of the Cold War South Africa was the powerhouse economy of Africa and they had made their own policies aimed at keeping it that way.

They did not respect the Portuguese authority and military, and clearly recognised the economic toll that conflicts in Guinea Bissau, Angola and Mozambique was taking on what was an impoverished small European country.

They had plenty of admiration for the Rhodesian forces but the South Africans had a long memory and remained suspicious. In spite of providing massive financial and military support they didn't ever formally recognise the country after Smith's UDI in November 1965.

Angola, Rhodesia and Mozambique quite simply were regarded as buffer states by South Africa, and economically and politically it was much cheaper and easier to support these countries than have to fund and cope with a war within their own borders.

With such diversity of interest, the usual track of forming open alliances was out of the question, but in anti-communism there was a common thread, and it was enough to bring the three parties together.

The secret agreement that resulted was known as 'Alcora' – *Aliança Contras as Rebliões em Africa* – alliance against communist rebels in Africa.

Initially the agreement was instigated by the intelligence agencies of the three countries, but this sharing of intelligence soon developed into a broader level of political and economic support and cooperation.

All this was explained to us by CIO chief Ken Flower as we sat in the back of a Rhodesian Air Force DC3 on the long flight to Luanda.

In the course of my SAS career I was party to two or three similar briefings by Ken Flower and I was always impressed with his knowledge and analysis. He was never shy of saying the unpopular truth and was a master of communication. Ken Flower was articulate and his unbiased and unemotional reasoning left no doubt in my mind that here was a man who was on top of his job – a true professional.

We liked true professionals in the SAS.

Ken had our attention as we listened to him, but for once I have to say it wasn't our usual undivided attention.

He had brought along with him a Portuguese-speaking staff member.

Paula Franks was stunningly built and beautiful and none of us could take our eyes off her. She sat next to him looking at us with a bulging blouse while he told his story.

'Mick,' he said, 'I asked your brigadier to put together a top tracker combat team. It is quite likely you will see some action against the Russian-backed MPLA terrorist group, but your main role is to show the *Paráquedistas* (their parachute regiment) how to operate in African bush conditions.

'The Portuguese have already put together some very good special operatives. Their *Flechas* – a mixed group of African trackers and Portuguese hunter bushmen – have proved they can find and infiltrate MPLA cells and communication lines, but the Portuguese cannot optimise this situation with troops capable of destructive follow-up action.

'Nothing wrong in general terms with the Paráquedistas,' he continued. 'The problem is they have all been trained for a European conflict in support of the NATO alliance. Conventional warfare is all they know, and as good at that as they may be it won't get them far in a guerrilla war being fought in the African bush.

'As part of the alliance we have agreed to help them by providing some expertise in bush warfare. You will be here for a month, most of which will be on operations with the Portuguese troops, but your Brigadier did mention you would probably want some base training time before venturing out on operations.'

'Yes Sir,' I replied. 'We think that is essential. We are dealing with professional soldiers of an elite regiment so we don't think it will take them long to adapt to our ways, but if we are to succeed, we need some time with them beforehand. A week would be good?'

'OK we can arrange that,' he replied.

'And Sir,' I continued, 'It would also be very good if we could have a Flecha group with us? We need to see how they operate – and so do the Paráquedistas. With both parties involved in the pre-deployment training I'm confident we'll make things happen.'

'Makes sense, Mick,' he replied. 'I'll organise that for you.'

The Brigadier had given me a general briefing before leaving base and said that five of us were to go to Angola.

Rex was a logical first choice because trackers didn't come much better than him and he was my right-hand man. I always worked Rex with Pig Dog who was not in the same league as a tracker but his powers of observation and instinct complemented Rex's skills. It made the two of them an incomparable lead scout pair. There were none better.

My own skills in the bush were more aligned with those of Pig Dog so with the three of us up front we backed ourselves on seeing or sensing danger before it saw us. That was our special talent.

I opted for Karate as number four in the team. He was another right-hand man to me and not far behind us in terms of tracking and bush craft.

My fifth and final choice was Cisco Guerra.

Cisco was a corporal, born of Portuguese parents and fluent with their language. Cisco would be essential for good communication with the troops in Angola. He wasn't a regular member of my own team but he was a good soldier and I was very happy to have him along.

That last point did however come into question as the DC3 rumbled through the sky towards Rundu in the Caprivi Strip where we would refuel before the final leg to Luanda.

Cisco did not hesitate to move in next to the gorgeous Paula. The two of them chatted away in Portuguese. Laughing at this and that and clearly enjoying each other's company.

We looked on unable to get a word in edgewise – and even if we did what could we say?

'Hi Paula. Obrigado!'

End of conversation because that was the only word of Portuguese the rest of us knew.

We landed in Luanda and initially stayed at an air force base. Here we were given two sets of Portuguese camouflage gear that we had to wear for the duration of our involvement with their forces. We all enjoyed the Portuguese clothing. It was made from a lighter material than our own and was very comfortable.

The following morning, we again boarded the DC3, this time to fly north-east of Luanda to a Portuguese military base at a place called Dundo close to the Congo border.

Ken Flower and the stunning Paula stayed in Luanda, and we were not slow to let Cisco know what a crying shame the rest of us thought that was.

As we approached our destination, I went forward to join the two pilots in the cockpit for a few minutes. I stood behind them looking out at the country we would be operating in.

And it was quite different to anything we'd been in before.

The land was very undulating, but the main difference was the many big open patches of grassland. These grassy areas were bordered by thickets of low woodland that formed corridors of cover around them, and that's where we'd stay. Crossing the grassy areas would be OK at night but in the day you'd be totally exposed and vulnerable.

Our operational success was to a large extent built on being invisible until we chose to strike. Whether or not we could get the Portuguese to follow suit was a big question, but we'd find out soon enough.

Dundo took me by surprise.

It was a much bigger place than I expected and not unlike Tete in Mozambique with a good-sized airport and adjacent military air base complex.

What also surprised me was the Paráquedistas being based here, but then it was explained they were in fact part of the Portuguese air force – not the army.

I didn't know if that was a good thing or a not-so-good thing, but I had misgivings. There was a voice in my head saying the air force have pilots, while soldiers rightfully belong to an army.

We were shown to a guest wing. It was basic but comfortable and there were ceiling fans that brought some relief from the heat and high humidity.

Once we had got ourselves sorted out, we were led to the operations room and introduced to Colonel Costa da Silva – the area commander.

The colonel was from Portuguese aristocracy and looked it.

He was a handsome man in his fifties. His glistening dark hair with silver streaks was combed back in waves that rested on his collar.

He greeted us in impeccable English and said how grateful and excited they were at having the SAS to assist them. I thanked him and introduced the team, pausing in front of Cisco and explaining we had brought him along as part of the training team but mainly to act as our communicator.

Cisco obliged by greeting the colonel in Portuguese and the two of them exchanged words for a short while.

The colonel turned back to me. 'This is excellent,' he said. 'I was concerned we may have trouble with language because none of the Paráquedistas speak much English.'

He then led us across the room and on one side of the staff officers was a group of nine smart and fit looking soldiers wearing green berets that had two jaunty thin green ribbons dangling down at the back. It looked very cool and very *latino* – I liked their style.

There was a major, a captain, three lieutenants, a warrant officer and three sergeants who made up the command element of D Company 21 BCP – *Batallião de Caçadores Paráquedistas.*

We smiled at each other and shook hands.

Next to the Paráquedistas sat an older man on his own.

He had a black beard and long hair that was brushed back and tied in a ponytail. He was rugged and tough looking and very dark. He'd either spent all his life out in the bush and sun, or else he had mixed blood – some Moorish content maybe? Maybe both?

'Meet Captain Marcelo Mariaga,' said the colonel. 'Marcelo is commander of the Flecha groups in this area.'

I shook his hand. He had a very firm grip and held it while also holding my arm with his left hand. He spoke in Portuguese then let me go.

The colonel interpreted.

'He says he is very happy you are here because there is much need for this training. His Flecha teams are good at finding the enemy and that is their job. To do their job it is important for them to remain anonymous. They seek but do not destroy – and that is the problem at the moment. They are finding the MPLA groups but most escape from the soldiers sent to deal with them. It is frustrating for the Flechas and things need to improve.'

I thanked the colonel and took Marcelo's hand again.

'Yes,' I said, 'I understand and we will do our best to fix that.'

The colonel then asked everyone to be patient for the next few minutes while he briefed us in English on the current situation.

He explained how the Angolan Communist Party merged with other dissident groups and formed the MPLA – the Movement for the National Independence of Angola – who were then trained and armed by the Russians.

The trouble started in earnest when over 4,000 insurgents led by Holden Roberto crossed into the northern province of the country from the Congo where they were based. An orgy of violence and destruction followed as they attacked farms, government outposts and trading centres, killing everyone they encountered, including women and children.

In surprise attacks, drunken and buoyed by belief in tribal spells they thought would make them immune to bullets, the attackers spread terror and destruction across a wide area. At least 1,000 Portuguese settlers and an unknown but considerably larger number of indigenous Angolans were slaughtered.

The Portuguese forces eventually responded and drove the rebels back across the border, inflicting heavy casualties on the MPLA who then split up and spread further east. From their bases in the thick Congo jungle they continued to launch periodic raids into Angola that were becoming increasingly frequent.

'To counter this,' the colonel continued, 'we have established what we call '*Frente Leste*' – the Eastern Front. This is a combined military and civil initiative aimed at protecting the local population and at the same time denying support to MPLA.

'We are steadily moving the locals into purpose-made villages where there is land to grow their crops and with facilities that will contribute to the economic and social development of their community. Facilities such as schools, medical centres, clean running water supplies and septic tank sewerage systems have been provided.

'The locals have responded well to this programme and to us in the military it means the MPLA no longer have access to scattered rural villages that were an easy source of logistical support and coercive recruitment.

'We can now also conduct an aggressive patrolling campaign in the bush areas along the border without worrying about civilian presence. This has been successful to a degree but as Marcelo explained we are not inflicting many casualties on the MPLA.'

As the colonel explained all this, I couldn't help thinking what our Brigadier had said about guerrilla warfare. He maintained that winning such conflicts required twenty per cent military effort and eighty per cent political effort.

The SAS had experience of this from Malaya and Oman, and certainly on this Eastern Front in Angola the Portuguese were working to the same equation.

I thanked the colonel as I moved to the front of the room.

My turn to do the talking, with Cisco standing next to me interpreting in Portuguese.

I started with some flattery.

'In C Squadron SAS we have several men from the British Parachute Regiment as well as some from the American 101st Airborne Division. Like you they were all trained for large-scale airborne assaults in a conventional war setting, but without exception they have adapted quickly and well to operating as Special Forces soldiers. We think that you, from the famous Parachute Rifle Battalion, will be the same.

'Unlike the noise of tanks, artillery and aircraft in a conventional war, our conflict is conducted in complete silence, at least until we are ready to strike. In our operations in Zambia, Mozambique and Rhodesia, our enemies have no idea they are facing an SAS Special Forces unit. They never see us. They don't know who we are or where we come from.

'We are an invisible force that can strike anywhere and there is nothing they can do about it.

'You will be the same, so from this moment D Company has a new name.

'You are *Os Fantasmas* – the ghosts. The ghosts of the Angolan bush!' I added with some emphasis.

There was some laughter as Cisco translated, but I could see they liked the idea.

'Os Fantasmas,' some of them repeated.

'In Zambia and Rhodesia especially, we often operate in big game country. We live with elephants, buffalo, lion, leopard and many other wild animals, and we test ourselves against them. We want to see or hear them before they know we are there.

'Knowing the animals and understanding the environment is critical to our survival and to avoid being compromised, but it also gives us a massive tactical advantage over our enemies.

'If we can live comfortably amongst lions, elephant and buffalo, there is no way we will ever be caught out by a bunch of people trained in Russia or China.

'It means we invariably take the enemy by surprise.

'We don't need to teach you about the animals. There isn't much game left in this area and you will be working with Flecha teams who know all about that anyway, but to make this concept work, and to best support the Flechas, your first requirement is to be silent.

'You have to learn to move through the bush without making a sound.

'You are Fantasmas. Ghosts that are neither seen nor heard.'

I let them chatter amongst themselves for a minute or two after this introduction and then moved in front of a small blackboard where I was pleased to see a selection of coloured chalk.

'Tomorrow morning,' I continued, 'we will teach you how to shoot and how to move when in action. It will be different to what you have been taught about fire fights, but to survive and to be successful in bush warfare it is essential you master these basics.

'Last year we ambushed a big group of Chinese-backed terrorists infiltrating into Rhodesia. It was a good ambush and many were killed, but we then found the tracks of another group that had bypassed our position and headed further inland where the country was steep and rocky.

'To catch up with them we used helicopters to leapfrog ahead on their tracks. Eventually we knew we were close to them, but because of the helicopters we also realised we had lost the element of surprise. The bush was thick and they would be waiting for us. We would be walking into their ambush.

'I was in front when suddenly a camouflaged figure popped up no more than ten metres in front of me. I felt the crack of the AK bullets as they flashed past my right ear, and then my brain registered that he was firing on automatic, and I knew that all rifles lift when firing on automatic.

'He'd had his chance. He'd missed me by inches and a second later he was dead, as my double tap blew his chest apart.'

As Cisco translated, I suddenly went down on one knee, my arms pointing towards them as if holding a rifle. 'Boom! Boom!' I shouted. To their astonishment I then dropped onto the floor, rolled off to my right, and came up again in the kneel. Again 'Boom! Boom!' as I gave then another two shots.

One of the lieutenants ducked for cover, while Marcelo stood up clapping. Rex and the boys could not control their laughter.

I stood up and apologised.

'Sorry about that,' I said, 'but consider the facts. The terrorist had the advantage of concealment and surprise. He initiated the action at very close range' – I paced out ten metres across the floor – 'He used half his thirty-round magazine.

'In contrast I was taken by surprise at very close quarters, and I only fired two rounds. So why is it that I am alive and he is dead?' I asked.

I paused for a second, casting my eyes over them while they caught up with my story from Cisco.

'Because he didn't know how to shoot and I did.

'That is why I am alive and talking to you today, and that is why we are going to spend time with you on the range.'

There was more animated chatter as I turned to the blackboard.

I glanced at the colonel and was pleased to see a big smile on his face. He was obviously enjoying this.

'Next we will show you the best and safest way to advance towards contact, or when under fire and closing with the enemy.

'We call it The Buddy System. You team up with a partner; the two of you look after each other and take it in turns to give cover while the other advances towards the enemy.

'You move forward just ten, fifteen, maybe twenty metres at a time depending on the ground.

'It means that at any given time you will only ever expose fifty per cent – half of your resource – while the other half watches in readiness or keeps the enemy occupied with fire while the other advances.'

I used the blackboard to illustrate the tactic and to also point out the need for strict adherence to 'channels' so as to avoid getting hit from behind by your own covering fire.

'Tomorrow we will start by practising this on the airfield without weapons, then later in the day we will do it at the shooting range with live firing. We will do this training every day so your men get used to working with their buddies and used to advancing with covering fire alongside.'

There were nods of approval as Cisco translated. I was happy they were understanding and appreciating our ways.

'Finally, later in the week, we will practise our attack techniques, but first we have to get the soldiers used to these basics that I have explained to you.'

I turned to the Colonel.

'Sir, I think that is enough talking from me for the moment. I am happy to answer any questions and then I'd like to work out a training programme with your team for the week. Once we have done that, I'd appreciate a guided tour of the base and surrounds so we can see the facilities and training areas. There is also some preparation work we need to do before we start.'

Colonel Costa da Silva was great to work with. He sat with us and the Paráquedistas while we worked out the timetable and training programme and helped with explanations of the routines they had established around the base and Dundo town.

Because of the heat and humidity, they habitually started before dawn, rested through the heat of the day, then continued their activities from around 1530 until after dark.

Unlike the Portuguese troops we had encountered in Mozambique they were proactive with defensive measures. Every day they patrolled the nearby Congo border with a Flecha group looking for tracks or any other sign of incursion, and there were both vehicle and foot patrols through and around the town. The base was well protected with machine gun pillbox positions made from sandbags, and there was a network of trenches for cover in the event of a rocket or mortar strike.

We were taken around the area in a Mercedes Unimog. I got Cisco to ask the driver if there was a shooting range, and we ended up going a couple of kilometres out of town on the road towards the Congo border.

It was fairly basic but would be fine for our needs. There were ten target frames and two firing points at 100 and 200 metres range.

'Mick, I've had an idea,' said Rex as we walked towards the stop banks.

'We should build a Jungle Lane. They will never have experienced anything like it and it will be good training for them.'

'Bloody great idea, Rex,' I replied immediately, 'but we've got eighty men to put through. We'll need to work out how we are going to do that.'

We sat down in the shade and I pulled out my notebook.

It didn't take long to work out that if we put them in pairs down a lane with ten targets it would take around twenty minutes per pair. If we built three lanes, we could get everyone through in around four and a half hours.

We jumped in the Unimog and headed towards the border looking for three suitable locations where the rifle fire would go in a safe direction, and we had no trouble finding them.

Back at the base I went to see the Colonel to get his clearance to conduct live firing training in the areas we had selected, and I was also hoping he could help us find some targets.

'Sir, we have decided it would be good for the Paráquedistas to experience what we call a Jungle Lane.

'In a suitable bush area, we position targets with varying degrees of concealment along a track. The targets are spread out over about 400 metres. We get the soldiers to follow the track and engage the targets with a rapid double tap as soon as they see them.

'The aim is to get them used to moving cautiously through the bush, and in the process we test their powers of observation, their reflexes and their shooting skills.

'We follow behind them to observe and count the hits on the targets, which we patch up as we go along. Because there are eighty men, we will put them through in pairs, and each run will take twenty minutes.

'This afternoon we found three good locations. Colonel, may I show you where these are on the map?' I asked. 'We want to be sure there are no problems with us live firing in these places.'

The Colonel had a look at the map and immediately gave us his approval.

'Thank you, Sir,' I said, 'and I have one final request. Do you have any shooting range targets here? We will need thirty for the Jungle Lanes.'

'We have,' he replied, 'but they have been well used and are now more patches than target. But we have a plane coming up from Luanda in the morning. We'll get them to bring in some new ones for you. What exactly do you want?'

'Twelve NATO figure 11 targets and eighteen of the smaller figure 12 targets would be ideal,' I replied. 'If they don't have the 12s we can make do with all 11s which they are bound to have.'

'Leave it with me,' he said.

The following morning, we met the Paráquedistas on the grassy edge of the airfield. They were dressed in boots, camo pants and dark green singlets, and they all looked to be in good shape.

Cisco told the Major we wanted them to get into pairs – the 'Buddy System' we had explained to them yesterday. He rattled off instructions and there was plenty of good-humoured banter as they sorted them-selves out.

We called for their attention as Rex and I demonstrated what we wanted them to do.

They watched in eager anticipation.

We gave a whistle to Cisco while Rex and I – about ten metres apart – went into the kneeling position with arms up as if handling a rifle.

Cisco gave a loud blast on the whistle and I shot forward as if starting a 100-metre dash. I kept low to the ground and, weaving from one side to the other, darted forward some twenty metres where I put down my arm, rolled over on the ground and came up in the kneeling position, aiming in front of me.

Rex followed a minute later and did the same, ending up about ten metres in front of me.

I exaggerated my movements to show them I was looking ahead, then once again burst forward.

Rex followed suit and then we stood up and returned to the assembled soldiers.

There was a buzz of excitement. The Major told Cisco it was what they called 'skirmishing', but they had never done it before.

He got the company spread out across the airfield and we split into three groups to control each platoon.

The whistles blew and the Portuguese soldiers leaped into action, full of enthusiasm and showing great commitment.

They dashed, weaved, tumbled and rolled from one end of the runway to the other. At the end we gave them a little time to get their breath back. There were smiles and animated chatter. They were enjoying it.

We blew the whistles again and off they went back to where we had started.

After cleaning up and breakfast we joined the Paráquedistas on the back of three big French Berliet trucks and headed to the shooting range about two kilometres away.

Everyone assembled on the 200-metre firing point where we had the next demonstration for them.

This time I put Karate and Pig Dog together. Both were deadly shots and had reflexes as fast as greased lightning.

They stood parallel with each other, about eight paces apart, rifles at the ready. I gave them the word and they started a slow advance towards the target.

I let them go for about twenty metres then blew the whistle.

As quick as a flash they dropped to the kneeling position, then 'Boom Boom' as they each fired a rapid double tap at the target.

We repeated the routine another four times, getting progressively closer to the target as we advanced.

My experienced ear noticed they were getting the shots away more quickly as we closed in. They didn't need as much time to aim at shorter range. It would only be a fraction of a second difference, but it all counts.

Karate and Pig Dog were exceptional, even by SAS standards, and the Paráquedistas watched on in awe.

After they had made their weapons safe I collected the target and took it back to the assembled soldiers. Karate and Pig Dog had each fired five double taps – ten rounds. I asked Cisco to count the holes in the target out loud in Portuguese.

As Cisco counted the last of twenty hits there were cries of amazement and admiration from the troops. They were all talking amongst themselves when one of the sergeants stepped forward towards me. He said something in Portuguese and everybody cheered.

I turned to Cisco.

'He says that if we can do this then so can the Paráquedistas!'

I looked back at him, smiling broadly and nodding my head in agreement.

We put twenty of them at a time through the range and kept going all morning until the Major finally called it quits.

At the start the firing was quick enough but it was wild, and the targets got off lightly. We worked on their technique and by the third time on the range they were getting the hang of it and scoring more hits.

As with the physical exercise earlier in the morning we were all impressed with their enthusiasm and commitment. When it's like this training is a breeze and highly enjoyable. We were having a good time too.

Before lunch I called in to see the colonel, firstly to update him on progress and secondly to enquire about the targets for the Jungle Lane.

The Major had seen him ahead of me and had given us a glowing report, so I didn't have to say much, but I did let him know how impressed we were with the Paráquedistas' response to the training.

The targets had arrived and he told me where I could pick them up.

In the afternoon we returned to the shooting range. This time the pairs would advance towards the targets, and on our signal one would fire at the target while the other dashed forward as we had done on the airfield in the early morning.

We gave them another demonstration, and satisfied all was well I left Cisco with the Major to handle things on the range. Meanwhile the four of us, with the targets, pulled ourselves up onto the back of one of the Berliets and asked the driver to take us to our Jungle Lane sites.

We marked each track with white tape hanging down from tree branches or bushes and along it concealed our targets in a variety of positions. At the start we made them relatively easy to see but increased the difficulty towards the last of the ten targets we positioned on each of the three lanes.

With everything set up we re-joined the troops and returned to camp. The Major let us know he thought it had been a day of excellent training.

'Thank you, Major,' I replied. 'Tomorrow we will again start with our physical training on the airfield, and then we have something special organised for you. We will be testing your movement through the bush, your powers of observation, your reactions, and your shooting skill.

'There is an excitement about this training I'm sure everyone will enjoy. I can still remember the excitement I had the first time I did a Jungle Lane on my Officer Training course.'

The following day before we left for the training, I explained how it would work and that because this was live firing training we would, for the sake of safety, be going to three different locations. Over the next day or two everybody would go through all three sites that had different challenges.

'We will put you through the courses two at a time. It will take between twenty minutes and half an hour. Once you have been through you can talk to your comrades but don't tell them any details. We want them to be as surprised as you were when they go through.'

There were nods of understanding as Cisco translated and we boarded the trucks.

For the next two days we put them through our Jungle Lanes and they couldn't get enough of it. Marcelo and his Flechas joined in everything, and some of his bushmen hunters were seriously good. He told me they had never had any formal training before so they were very excited at being included in the programme.

Of the three lanes, the one Karate and Pig Dog had built was the firm favourite. The talking point was a full-size figure 11 target they had laid flat on the ground totally concealed behind a tree. But they had attached a length of brown string to the top of the target, run it over a horizontal branch about two metres off the ground, and led it back some ten metres on the side of the track.

As the pair of Paráquedistas approached, Pig Dog would hang back and take up the end of the string. On a signal from Karate he would then pull the string and the target would pop up, swinging and rotating, just two or three metres in front them.

They laughingly told us afterwards that several soldiers got such a fright they shouted out Portuguese expletives we'd been quick to learn, and one of them had half emptied his magazine at the target before Karate intervened and stopped him firing off the other half.

On the second afternoon the Colonel came down to join us and to participate on one of the lanes.

'Our Brigadier joins us quite frequently on this sort of training,' I told him.

'He really enjoys it but always tells the Training Officer what score he wants before starting.'

'Ha! Your Brigadier is a wise man, Mick,' he said laughing but at the same time looking pointedly at me.

'No problem, Sir,' I replied. 'We will ensure you have a very creditable score. It's the least we can do. You have been a great help to us.

'OK. Cock your weapon and take off the safety catch. Follow the white markers and be prepared. You're on your own now and there are ten MPLA waiting for you.'

Rex and I grinned at each other. Nobody knew the rules of engagement better than we did.

Returning to base on the truck the troops started singing. They were in high spirits, not just because of the training but also because it was Saturday night. The beer and spirits would flow and there would be more singing, because tomorrow, Sunday, was a rest day.

Some would go to church, some would play football, and then they would spend the day cleaning their clothes and equipment.

After cleaning up we had a spicy chicken dinner with the Colonel, washed down with delicious chilled Casal Garcia Vino Verde. As the end of dinner approached, we could hear singing from in front of the troops' kitchen.

'Have you ever listened to Fado singing?' asked the Colonel.

He went on to explain it was an old traditional form of Portuguese music with songs that could be about anything, happy or sad, but they all had simple easy-to-follow choruses which everybody joined in.

He suggested we go and join the soldiers.

We sat on the steps outside the canteen with the soldiers in groups around us. Three of them had guitars and were capable musicians.

The Major disappeared for a few minutes, returning with a bottle containing a clear spirit with a brown twig in it. He passed round small glasses. The Colonel toasted us and downed the glass. We all followed suit.

I gasped as the liquid burned my mouth and throat, but it was delicious.

The Major topped up our glasses with more anise.

As the warmth of the alcohol swept through our bloodstream, we firstly found ourselves foot-tapping with the Fado, and then eventually joining in with some of the less complicated choruses.

The troops meanwhile had picked up the tempo and some started folk dancing.

Eventually there was a break in the party, while more *cerveja* – the second handy word of Portuguese I'd learned – was opened.

One of the guitarists stood up and called for everyone's attention. He rattled off something in Portuguese and everybody cheered.

'This next song is for the SAS,' said Cisco.

There was a moment of silence while the three guitarists conferred, followed by a bit of string tuning, and then they started:

> *I saw the light on the night that I passed her window.*
> *I saw the flickering shadow of love on her blind.*
> *She was my woman...*
> *As she deceived me I watched and went out of my mind...*

And then the bit we had all been waiting for:

My, my, my Delilah!
Why, why, why Delilah!

The sparkling Angolan night sky lifted a little on its hinges as seventy-five Paráquedistas and five SAS men blasted Tom Jones's best song out into the atmosphere.

Like our Jungle Lanes they couldn't get enough of it.

After the third time and another couple of anise drinks, Rex, Cisco and I decided to call it a night. It had been a great one, but I wanted to do some recce work in the morning, looking for areas suitable for the next training phase.

Karate and Pig Dog had moved in next to a couple of the sergeants and Marcelo. I noticed another bottle being passed round. The Fado was back in full swing, and as I approached our quarters Tom Jones again filled the air.

My, my, my Delilah!!
Why, why, why Delilah!!

And while all this was going on two men – PIDE secret police – were heading towards Dundo in an elderly black diesel Mercedes. They had news for us about a big MPLA camp.

We'd find out soon enough how good our training had been.

Haunting the MPLA

A little over sixty kilometres to the east of Dundo the small settlement of Chitato was rapidly expanding.

Diamonds had been discovered and a Portuguese mining company had moved in. On top of that Chitato was a resettlement centre, part of the Portuguese 'Eastern Front' project, and now there was a school and a hospital. Hundreds of locals had moved into the basic housing provided and either found employment at the mine or grew crops in the fertile alluvial soils alongside the nearby Chiumbe River.

It was a convenient location for PIDE – the Portuguese secret police, the equivalent of our Special Branch – to run sources that could report on any MPLA activity across the Congo border that was just twelve kilometres away to the north.

On the day of our Jungle Lane training with the Paráquedistas an African man and his wife walked into the Chitato police station. The man explained they came from the settlement of Miumba, about ten kilometres across the Congo border almost due north of Chitato.

He and his wife had been on their way to the local general store when they were confronted by a gang of six armed MPLA terrorists.

'They were very drunk,' he said, 'and as we approached, two of them grabbed my wife. I tried to intervene but the others overpowered me and I was severely beaten. As I lay unconscious the gang repeatedly raped my wife. When they had finished with her, they beat her and said they would be coming back for more. They left us both injured and lying on the ground.

'After some time, other people helped us and we managed to get home. We gathered our possessions and left our house.

'We have come here to escape the MPLA and we hope to settle in one of your new villages.'

The couple were passed on to the PIDE operatives and were questioned in detail about the MPLA.

They told the PIDE men that immediately south of Miumba, no more than a kilometre away, there was a collection of bare rocky outcrops with

Haunting the MPLA   69

thick woodland and streams between them. The MPLA had taken over some old farm buildings at the foot of these hills and had built a training camp.

They said the MPLA numbers had steadily increased in recent weeks and now there were at least one hundred. Every day they came in to the settlement of Miumba to get food and millet beer. They showed no respect for the locals and there had been several incidents like the one they suffered.

While drinking they had been heard talking about how they were going to take the diamonds at Chitato.

The PIDE men listened with interest. They had heard of MPLA threats to raid the diamond fields before, but with a hundred of them now just twenty-two kilometres away this was clearly more than just another rumour.

They jumped into their old Mercedes and headed towards Dundo.

I'd just finished an early breakfast with Rex and we were about to head out of camp when we were called to the Operations Room. There we found the Colonel and the Paráquedistas Major with two other men we learned were the PIDE operatives from Chitato.

We were told about the MPLA camp near Miumba.

'We have our own thoughts on how to deal with this situation,' said Colonel da Silva, 'but do you mind sharing with us what you would be doing if you had just received such news?'

'No problem, Sir,' I replied. 'Isn't that why we are here?

'I would immediately send an air reconnaissance request to the air force. With air photographs we can see exactly what we are up against, and more importantly the ground conditions both at the target and on the approaches to the target. With that information we can then make a realistic assessment on how to approach the target without compromise and how best to attack it once we are there.'

'Very good,' said the Colonel, 'but we don't have Canberras.'

'But we do, Sir,' I replied. 'The SAS are here, so this is an SAS operation, and the Rhodesian Airforce will support SAS operations wherever they may be. I'll make the request through the SAS. That way we'll avoid the diplomatic channels that are bound to get in the way if you go formally through Luanda.'

The Colonel laughed and shook his head. 'I'm not going to turn down that offer. What do we need to make it happen?' he asked.

I looked at Karate.

'Comms,' I said. 'We brought an HF radio set with us but we'll need some help with rigging it up to an aerial that will get through to our base.'

Karate nodded in agreement while the Colonel called his Signals Officer.

An hour later Karate tapped out a coded Morse message with details of the MPLA camp and a request for a high-altitude photo-recce run. The SAS duty operator back in Rhodesia told us to stay on air and that Sunray would have an answer for us within the hour.

I pictured the Brigadier back at base shaking his head at the request for reconnaissance of a site that would be at least two thousand kilometres away.

'And would you like some ice-cream as well, Mick?' I imagined him saying to himself as he picked up the phone to call Ken Flower. We'd definitely need CIO support to get the air force to agree to the mission.

'...diditdit, diditdit, dahdedah,' ended the reply as it came through just over an hour later.

It was short and sweet.

The Canberra would take the pictures that morning.

We let the Colonel know. He was excited and had many questions I couldn't answer.

'How will they get the information to us?' he asked.

It was a reasonable question and one in my mind as well so all I could think of saying was it wasn't our problem. The Brigadier would work out a way to get it to us.

Meanwhile I wanted to return to talking about the attack.

'Our usual tactic with camp attacks is to infiltrate at night. We have an assault group that stays short of the camp itself while most of our force encircles the camp in ambushing 'Stop Groups'. Just before first light the assault group advances through the camp, flushing out the terrorists who will flee towards the waiting stop groups.

'The assault group has the element of surprise so will inflict casualties, but most kills will be made by the stop groups.

'The problem with taking on a camp of this size and with over one hundred terrorists is that the effect of the assault group is limited to its immediate area. Terrorists at the opposite end of the camp have time to escape unscathed, and with such numbers the stop groups cannot get them all. Many will escape.

'To get the optimum result we need fire power to engage the deeper parts of the camp while the assault group advances. That fire power can be helicopter gunships if they are available, but generally we use our own mortar teams because they can walk in with us and set themselves up in complete silence.

'As the assault group advances the mortars pound the camp ahead of them. It's devastating and will result in many more casualties.'

I explained all this with help from Cisco interpreting and with diagrams on a whiteboard.

There followed a long conversation in Portuguese between the Colonel and the Paráquedista officers, and while that was on-going Karate came into the room and handed me a bit of paper.

It was a message from the Brigadier. The air photographs would be delivered to us tomorrow afternoon around 1300hrs. They were being sent by air mail – Canberra bomber air mail! He would be on the flight and if we had any requests, we were to let him know.

While Karate went back to the radio to acknowledge, I shared the news with the others.

'Excellent news, Mick,' said the Colonel. 'We were discussing your camp attack tactics and can see the wisdom in using additional fire power. The problem is we don't have anything like that here. The Paráquedistas have a heavy mortar platoon but they are in Lisbon. We will have to make do with the assault group. Perhaps we should advance through the camp faster than usual?' he asked.

'Yes, Sir. We could do that,' I replied.

I'd no sooner got the words out of my mouth than Rex suddenly leaned forward and grabbed my arm.

'The Canberra, Mick!' he said. 'Ask the boss to bring in a couple of our own tubes and maybe forty bombs. They will easily fit into the bomb bay.'

My face lit up.

'Rex, you're a bloody genius,' I said.

For the remainder of the morning we took the Paráquedistas out onto the airfield and walked them through the routine of encircling a terrorist camp. We drilled into them the need to be totally silent, to stay concealed and to use double taps – 'Boom Boom' – when firing.

Midway through this the Colonel called me over. He had Marcelo with him.

'Mick,' he said, 'we have briefed Marcelo on the situation and he is very keen to help us. His Flechas are not combat troops but as you would have seen on your Jungle Lane training, they are exceptional bushmen. Marcelo has suggested they go ahead of you and send out a small recce team – just two or three men – to locate the camp.

'They will not risk compromise by getting too close, but they will work out how best to reach the camp. They will return and guide you in on the night of the attack.'

It took me by surprise but it didn't take long for me to see the value in this. The men involved would be African hunters and trackers. We took pride in being invisible in the bush. These men had been living like that all their lives.

I accepted at once and decided to push my luck.

I explained to Marcelo that one of the more difficult parts of these camp attacks was leading the stop groups around the back of the camp in the dark. Perhaps his men could have a look at that as well?

Marcel was delighted.

'We are part of this now,' he said to the Colonel. 'The Flechas will not fail you.'

The following afternoon we all rushed outside excitedly as the Canberra did a low pass over the Dundo runway.

The big bomber climbed away then circled round for landing. We watched as the landing lights came on, and the undercarriage dropped as the aircraft descended in front of a swirling haze of super-heated air and exhaust gases.

We covered our ears as the glistening green and brown Canberra taxied towards us and stopped.

The jet engine noise wound down and a side door opened. A step ladder was pushed out to the ground.

First out was the Brigadier.

He put on his sand coloured SAS beret, and once satisfied with its position walked towards the waiting entourage. I stepped forward and saluted. He returned the compliment then shook my hand.

'Good to see you, Mick,' he said.

I introduced him to the Colonel who then did the honours of introducing the Paráquedistas.

While I was busy with these introductions, I'd not noticed another sand coloured beret that had descended from the Canberra. There was a tap on my shoulder.

'Hello, Mick,' said Sergeant Pete Coles. 'I suppose a salute would be in order,' he said with a big grin on his face.

'The boss thought you might appreciate a bit of help with the mortars,' he said.

Pete Coles was our new mortar platoon sergeant. He'd joined us from the British Parachute Regiment. Pete was a low intensity professional. Nothing seemed to faze him, and when it came to using the mortars, we'd never had anyone who came even close to matching his expertise.

With Pete and two 81mm mortar tubes the MPLA were now in serious trouble.

I left Karate and Pig Dog to help the Canberra crew unload the mortars and bombs, while the rest of us headed towards the operations room.

The Brigadier took four black and white air photographs from a large brown envelope and spread them out on the table.

We all gathered round, craning our necks to see the target.

'It's a big camp,' he said. 'It covers roughly four hundred square metres, and judging from the number of buildings and shelters we estimate there are between 120 and 150 MPLA in residence.

'What particularly caught our attention were these,' he said pointing to an open area with objects that we couldn't make out, until he put an enlargement in front of us.

'Mortars,' he said. 'There are eight 82mm mortars in this picture. You mentioned they planned to attack a nearby town. With these weapons they will do massive damage to an unsuspecting and unprepared civilian population. Once they have flattened the place with mortars they will descend on the town and kill off any survivors they find. Then there will be an orgy of looting and plunder. It will be like Holden Roberto all over again.'

'But more serious this time,' interjected the Colonel, 'because Chitato is a diamond town.'

The Brigadier's eyes lit up.

'So that's what this is all about. The Russians will be behind this. The MPLA can have Angola but the Russians want the oil and the diamonds. Mick, with over 100 terrorists to take on, your request for these pictures would always have been approved, but now I'm especially glad it happened and that you asked for the mortars.

'Chitato won't stand a chance if the MPLA attack. When do you plan on taking out the camp?' he asked.

I waited to see if the Colonel would reply to that but he just looked at me.

'First light day after tomorrow,' I said.

He nodded. 'Let's hope the MPLA don't jump the gun.'

The Canberra crew had refuelled and were keen to go, but the Colonel insisted they first have lunch. He brought out several bottles of wine that were politely declined.

'Can't drink and drive,' said the Brigadier.

'Unfortunately,' he added, while wistfully eying the chilled Casal Garcia.

But they wouldn't let them leave empty handed. As we left the dining room the Colonel gave the Brigadier and the three Canberra crew members a bottle wrapped in white tissue paper. I spotted a brown twig at the top of one of the bottles. If the aircraft got short of fuel on the way home, the four of them were carrying an immediate solution.

Pete Coles had added twelve smoke bombs to the forty high explosive units we had ordered for the attack. He wanted to see how the heat and humidity of this region affected the flight of the bomb and his aiming.

We discussed what to do.

Firstly, I made Karate and Pig Dog the firing team. They had both done mortar training and were good operators. They would understand and implement the commands from Pete.

I asked the Colonel for two volunteers from the Paráquedistas to assist the two of them by passing the bombs to be fired. All I wanted was speed. As a bomb was fired, they should have another waiting to go immediately. We needed rapid fire. We couldn't give the MPLA time to escape.

I would do the forward fire control as I would be leading the assault group with the Paráquedista Major. Pete didn't want much from me, just the initial correction after the first two bombs. Once confirmed on target he would switch one tube to fire on the outer extremities of the camp. He'd then adjust fire so the barrage slowly crept back in towards the centre of the camp.

Meanwhile the other tube would maintain the strike against the other end of the camp, and then also advance a creeping barrage towards the centre.

Escape and evasion exercise participants, 1969. Brigadier centre, author second on his right.

(*Above*) Parachute course, 1969.
Author back row, second from
left, standing next to Fish on
crutches with a sprained ankle.

(*Left*) Author helicopter
training.

(*Right*) Helicopter training with the French-built Alouette 3.

(*Below*) May 1969. Author receiving SAS wings and beret from Rhodesian Minister of Defence Jack Howman.

(*Above left*) SAS parachute exercise while still using the old British 'X' type 28' flat canopy parachutes. It was a good day in mid-1969 when we upgraded to the American 32' shaped canopy T10s.

(*Above right*) Jumping with equipment.

C Squadron SAS in Malaya.

(*Above left*) C Squadron patrol kit, Malaya.

(*Above right*) Smoke break, C Squadron, Malaya.

SAS officers had to be as competent as everybody else on all the weapons we used.

(*Above left*) Inspirational Mike Higgins on patrol.

(*Above right*) General Peter Walls – first commander of C Squadron SAS.

Air orientation course. Author centre with SAS beret.

(*Right*) Grandparents Frederick and Beatrice Graham.

(*Below*) Author with P.K. van der Byl, Rhodesian Minister of Defence.

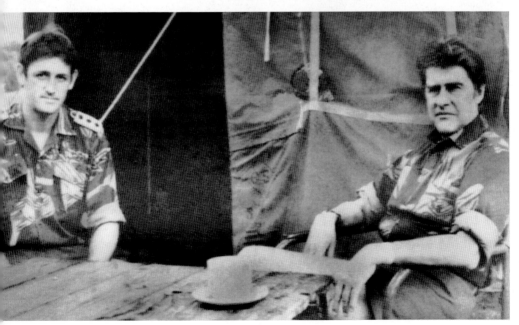

Parents Frederick Walter and Joan Graham.

Pig Dog on left.

Tupolev Tu-134 similar to the one that crashed killing Frelimo leader Samora Machel.

Lebombo Mountains where the Tupolev crashed.

(*Above*) Rhodesian Air Force Canberra bomber.

(*Left*) One of the many massive 'Inselbergs' in the Nampula province of Mozambique where the SAS hunted Frelimo.

(*Above*) Mozambique village of Cuamba where we were in hot pursuit of a local Frelimo gang.

(*Right*) Henry Munyaradzi's soapstone 'Marina'.

(*Above left*) Russian-backed MPLA terrorist leader Eduardo Mondlane.

(*Above middle*) Chinese-backed ZANU terrorist leader Robert Mugabe.

(*Above right*) Chinese-backed Frelimo terrorist leader Samora Machel.

(*Left*) SAS Sabre Land Rover.

(*Below*) Fish checks out the river before crossing.

The Belgian-made 'FN' 7.62mm self-loading rifle was unsurpassed in the African environment.

Bridge demolitions with Renamo in Mozambique.

Training with captured communist weapons.

Dave Berry, killed on an 'unauthorised mission' according to the South African Defence Force chiefs.

A cold looking author standing far left with Dave Berry centre. We had just been recovered from an extended operation in Mozambique.

Carrying AKs and RPDs became common practice in the SAS.

On patrol.

'A handful of hard men'.

The final salvos would be close together, concentrated in the centre of the camp.

With this expertise I decided to hold the assault until Pete had fired off all the mortar bombs. We'd sit in our positions and act as another stop group – ready to take out any MPLA fleeing the mortar attack and heading in our direction.

Later that afternoon we went away from the barracks to test our mortars and practise the attack. I asked the Major to bring everyone along to watch the show and understand what would be happening for real on the day after tomorrow.

We picked a target we could all see in the distance, and worked out the range and bearing on the map. Pete and the boys set up the tubes with enthusiastic help from the two Paráquedista volunteers.

Watching through my binoculars I saw the first two smoke bombs erupt on our target.

'Short!' I shouted. 'Add one hundred! Left one hundred!'

Pete repeated the commands. Karate and Pig Dog adjusted elevation and direction. The Paráquedistas handed them another two bombs that were soon whistling towards the target.

'Crump! Crump!' as they exploded.

'On target! Fire for effect!' I shouted, and Pete took over.

We only had six smoke bombs for each tube but it was patently obvious to everyone watching that what Pete was going to do with the high explosive would be devastating.

The excitement and eager anticipation of the Paráquedistas was tangible. For many this would be their first taste of action. We kept reminding them about composure. The Portuguese are a noisy race and keeping them quiet until the start was my biggest fear.

At 1600 hours the following afternoon we left Dundo. The convoy was led by the Major in a command and signals Unimog, we were on one of the three Berliet trucks that followed, and finally a Unimog ambulance brought up the rear.

Including the Unimogs was a good move by the Major.

If we had casualties, they could drive cross country right up to the camp, and he'd ordered them to do that as soon as they heard the mortars open fire.

The sixty-five kilometres to the border north of Chitato took us an hour and a half.

Marcelo and his Flechas were waiting for us on the side of the road.

He'd sent out two recce parties. The first closed in on the camp itself while the other group circled round behind it to recce the stop positions.

I called Cisco and Pete and we went to speak to Marcelo. We showed him the map and the location of where we had proposed to site the mortars – about 1,200 metres short of the camp. The map showed a small stream and just beyond that what looked like flat open country.

Cisco explained that for the mortars to be effective it was critically important for us to be sure of our base plate location.

Marcello nodded in understanding and called over two of his African Flechas. He showed them the map and explained the situation. They had no hesitation in recognising the stream and assured us they would take us to that exact spot.

We split into two groups.

The Major, Rex, Cisco and I with twenty Paráquedistas made up the assault group, along with the five-man mortar team. The Paráquedistas each carried two mortar bombs.

The stop groups consisted of the remaining fifty Paráquedistas that would give us twenty-five two-man ambush positions behind the camp. We watched them march away into the gloom, led by two of Marcelo's Flechas.

Marcelo joined his two trackers at the front of our column as we started the slow walk in towards the camp. We had nine kilometres to go.

I'd explained to Marcelo and the Major the need for going slow when moving at night and to make sure everybody stayed connected.

The only sound came from tiny Scops owls purring in the trees as we made our way slowly forward. There was no moon but the sky was illuminated by a glowing Milky Way and a million surrounding stars. The Plough was as bright as I have ever seen it and we followed its front stars that pointed due north.

And the Paráquedistas were quiet.

It took us four hours to reach the mortar position. Pete was happy with the location. We unloaded all the bombs we had carried in, checked VHF radio comms and then we left him and his team to set up the tubes.

Marcelo's amazing guides led us forward towards the camp.

We stopped. One of the Flechas beckoned Marcelo and whispered something to him.

'How close do you want to go?' was the question translated by Cisco.

'Show me,' I replied.

We asked the Major to stay where they were while Cisco, Marcelo and I followed the guide. After about fifty metres I could make out the form of thatched shelters and a building roughly another fifty metres further on.

Fifty metres was close but there was cover in the form of low bushes and medium sized trees.

The Major and the rest of the group joined us. We had plenty of time so the Major and I put the men into pairs and spread them out along the edge of the camp. It was a chance for him to say a last few words to them before the action started.

I heard him say '*Os Fantasmas*' a couple of times and enjoyed that.

The haunting of the MPLA by the ghosts of Angola was now just a few hours away.

With everyone spread out to our satisfaction, all we had to do was wait.

I'd still not heard a sound from the Paráquedistas.

I wondered how the stop groups were getting on.

Nothing I could do about it, so no point worrying and I'd been massively impressed with the Flechas. If they could do the same with the stop groups as they had done with us, there would be no problems.

The hours towards dawn dragged unbearably and I'm sure most of our attacking force nodded off. Marcelo was in a deep sleep on the ground next to me, but it didn't matter.

We were in position. The trap was set.

Faint lines of light started to appear in the east, and some birds started singing. I let the Major know we were about to start the action.

I gave the VHF radio a couple of clicks to alert Pete, then used the whisper mike.

'Open fire!' I ordered.

A few moments later we heard the distant booming as the first two bombs were fired. There was a period of silence then suddenly the screaming arrival of the bombs.

'Crump! Crump!' as they exploded.

'On target, but go left 100!' I shouted into the radio.

Moments later thirty-eight high explosive bombs were raining down on the camp complex.

A group of five or six MPLA ran towards us.

'Boom Boom,' as the Major took one out with a good double tap. We followed suit and they were all down.

We heard the sound of double taps coming from along our assault line and then from further away in the higher ground to the north. That would be the stop groups in action.

'Boom Boom'. We'd taught the Paráquedistas how to shoot. I had a little smile to myself. How good was that.

The mortars eventually stopped firing. The bombardment only lasted three or four minutes but it would have seemed an eternity to the MPLA caught in the open with sleep still in their eyes.

I asked the Major to order the advance.

I darted forward about twenty metres and knelt behind a small bush. I fired double taps into three thatched shelters in front on me. A figure darted away from the furthest, but only made two or three metres before another double tap did its work.

The Major was alongside me, about five metres to my left. He too was busy with targets. Marcelo came up to join him as Cisco moved in on my right. Before moving again, I had a quick look at the assault line and was pleased to see the Paráquedistas moving in a good disciplined formation, firing double taps, aggressive and determined.

It took some time but eventually we reached the camp extremities and I called a halt. I explained to the Major that we should now retreat back to where we had started the assault, and allow the stop groups to sweep in towards the camp.

I asked him to make sure everyone was connected with their neighbours and to advance as we had done through the camp. I explained there could be survivors hiding and waiting for us to show ourselves. They should advance with caution.

Cisco explained and the Major rattled off orders to the Platoon Commanders who would lead the sweep.

We knelt down on the ground, watching and waiting as they closed in on us. There were a few bursts of gunfire, then eventually the Major announced they were all safely at the edge of the camp. He kept in constant radio contact until at last we saw them approaching. We all stood up and waved and I finally relaxed. We'd joined up without accident or incident.

I heard vehicles approaching and turned around to see the two Unimogs making their way slowly towards us. Pete and his mortar team were on the back of the ambulance vehicle.

I asked the Major if he would get the troops into a defensive position around us, and then the first priority was to have a brew and some breakfast. We'd then start searching the camp and gathering up the weapons and anything that might be of interest to the PIDE police.

We recovered the eight 82mm mortars and found boxes of bombs under the rubble of a mudbrick building that had been hit by our mortars. We put those on the back of the Unimog with Pete's crew.

In addition, we recovered eighty-two AKM assault rifles, and twenty older Semenov SKS carbines along with several boxes of the 7.62 mm intermediate ammunition used by both weapons.

The body count was eighty-seven dead.

The Major was busy inside his signals vehicle relaying the news back to the Colonel as we all started the walk back towards the border and our waiting trucks.

It had been a long night and a big night, so unsurprisingly the men were tired and quiet, but we knew that would soon change once they'd cleaned up and had a rest.

We got back to Dundo around 1300 hours and headed for the showers and our bunks. The Colonel didn't interfere but ordered a debrief in the operations room at 1730 hours.

The Colonel congratulated everybody as we filed into the operations room.

The Major kicked off by saying how amazing Marcelo's Flecha guides had been with his Platoon Commanders when positioning the stop groups. They could not have done that without them, he said. His praise continued for Marcelo and the guides that led the assault group. Cisco translated for me and at an appropriate time I stood up and applauded, agreeing with everything he'd said.

The Major had high praise for his men, who were outstanding, and I agreed whole-heartedly with that as well, and finally he had high praise for our SAS team who he said had led them on this very successful mission.

It was my turn to speak and I kept it short.

I told them how I looked up when moving forward in the assault and how happy I was to see the Paráquedistas advancing and shooting as we had taught them. But most of all, I said, I was impressed with them keeping quiet. I didn't hear a sound at any time during the attack, and I told them frankly that I hadn't been expecting that. I thanked them for their commitment and professionalism and expressed our pleasure at working with such a fine body of men.

The Colonel translated for the others, then turning to me with a smile on his face told me I could expect to hear plenty from the Paráquedistas that night.

As the celebrations intensified it was just a matter of time before it happened.

There was a lull in the noise as whispers passed from one group to the next.

Then the three guitarists led the way:

> *I saw the light on the night that I passed her window.*
> *I saw the flickering shadow of love on her blind*
> *Sheeeee was my woman…*
> *As she deceived me, I watched and went out of my mind…*
> *My, my, my Delilah!*
> *Why, why, why Delilah!*

The Aftermath

The camp attack had a profound effect on the MPLA. The loss of the cell created ructions within the organisation. They splintered and became increasingly impotent.

On top of that the Portuguese strategy in what they called the *Frente Leste* had won the hearts and minds of the local population. Aggressive border patrolling by the Paráquedistas and Flechas guaranteed their security in the new settlements, where they prospered.

By early 1970 the Portuguese had won the war in Angola.

With political stability, oil in Cabinda, and diamonds found in the north-eastern areas, Angola went from strength to strength. Luanda developed into a colourful and prosperous city.

The tragedy for Angola was that the good times only lasted until 1974.

The Portuguese had not been doing so well in Mozambique, and even worse in Guinea-Bissau. The Portuguese population back in Lisbon had had enough. President Caetano was ousted in a coup led by General Spinola – the 'Carnation Revolution' leaders immediately ordered all Portuguese troops serving overseas back home.

In Angola they appointed a temporary military government tasked with handing over the country to a coalition of three identified pro-independence movements: the MPLA, UNITA and the FNLA.

The Russians were quick to increase support to the MPLA and pushed them into occupying the oil-rich Cabinda province.

With the smell of oil in their nostrils the American CIA jumped into the fray with backing for UNITA.

Hostilities between the two factions increased.

The Russians responded by sending in the Cubans – their colonial troops – and equipped them with heavy weaponry and MiG fighters.

The USA responded by backing an invasion by their new-found friends in South Africa. The South Africans had superb, highly mobile vehicles specifically designed for conflict in Africa, and they had French Mirage fighters that soon achieved air superiority.

The Russians reinforced the Cubans with more modern weaponry and the latest MiG fighters that nullified the initial advantage achieved by the South African Mirages.

By 1980 the MPLA were winning on the battlefields, and with USA fears of getting involved in another Vietnam, they and the South Africans pulled out of the conflict.

With the country now in their hands the MPLA set about dealing with internal factions that had developed during the conflict. Following the example of China, North Korea, and Vietnam, a purge was initiated to eliminate all suspected followers and sympathisers of 'orthodox communism' inside and outside the party.

The Cubans supported the purge with barbaric enthusiasm. Nobody will ever know exactly how many innocent Angolans were slaughtered in this meaningless exercise but figures released after the civil war suggested as many as 200,000 perished.

It's not hard to understand why we in the SAS had no time for the senseless ideology of communism.

Relentless Pursuit

Some of our SAS operations took us into places with spectacular scenery but none could compare with one in the Nampula province of Mozambique where, not for the first time, we were after a marauding Frelimo terrorist gang.

Portuguese Colonel Costa Da Silva had been very successful in Angola with his Eastern Front policy – a combination of a hearts and minds campaign with the local population, some aggressive military patrolling, and action that together won the war against the MPLA.

As a result of his success he had been moved to Nampula in Mozambique where it was hoped he could do the same against Frelimo.

It was a vain hope and typical of the edicts that came from a very out-of-touch Lisbon.

It was a vain hope for a number of reasons:

Firstly, Frelimo were being trained and armed by the Chinese – not the Russians – as was the case with the MPLA in Angola. The Russians didn't have anything like Mao's *Little Red Book* that remains the blueprint for guerrilla warfare to this day. The Chinese even supplied their own political commissars to operate with the terrorist groups in the field, keeping them focussed, making sure they strictly followed the ideology.

Secondly, by the time Colonel Costa Da Silva took command in northern Mozambique, Frelimo were already well established and in control of the Cabo Delgado and Niassa provinces to the north of Nampula. They had free access from bordering Tanzania where the training camps were based, and with virtually no Portuguese military presence they became Frelimo's first 'Liberated Areas'.

Thirdly, in Angola the Colonel had the well trained *Paráquedistas* – the parachute regiment – to work with. In contrast, in Mozambique he had inexperienced, barely trained national service conscripts. And it was very much a passive military presence. There was no aggressive patrol regime. They were happy to let Frelimo have free rein in the bush around their small garrisons.

The Colonel had received increasing complaints from local settlers about attacks around the small town of Gurue. There had been ambushes on the roads and land mines laid that had killed local farmers and their families. There was a garrison in the town but the soldiers achieved nothing.

Gurue was important to Mozambique. It was situated due west of Nampula and less than 100 km from the border with Malawi. Although only 15° south of the equator, it was situated amongst high mountains and enjoyed a cool and wet microclimate.

That made it ideal for growing tea, and a number of plantations had been established. It was a prosperous, thriving community that made a useful contribution to the economy of Mozambique.

With the sudden arrival of Frelimo all this was now under threat, and Colonel Costa Da Silva had to do something about it.

He called the Portuguese Embassy in Salisbury and asked if the SAS could help him again.

Because Frelimo were actively assisting Rhodesian terrorist group ZANU there was never any high-level reluctance to give us the go-ahead with these missions, and as a result my SAS team, Sierra One Seven, was given the task of providing that assistance.

We met the Brigadier in the operations room where he'd organised map coverage of the area around Gurue.

The maps were extraordinary; we'd never seen anything like them before.

In between relatively flat areas were individual mounds of closely spaced orange coloured contour lines, and there were dozens of them right across the map.

We all knew that the closer the contour lines the steeper the hill slope, and some of them were so close together they merged into a solid thick line, indicating what would be an almost vertical slope.

'They are called *Inselbergs*,' explained the Brigadier, 'and there are so many in this area it is called an Inselberg Plain. It's remarkable and I guess they were all created at the time when the rift valley and nearby Lake Malawi were being formed.

'*Inselberg* is a German word meaning Island Mountain, and it is a good description because these massive granite features rise abruptly from the surrounding plains and look like islands in the middle of the ocean.

'The other point I have established for your planning purposes is that this area is high – over 5,000 feet – and many of these inselbergs rise for another 2,000 feet. As a result, the area is generally cool and has significantly more rainfall. Given it is early February you are bound to be caught in the rain at some stage, so be prepared for that.

'Initially we will be flying to Nampula for a briefing on the situation by Colonel Costa Da Silva, and then we will fly to Gurue where there is a commercial airfield. We will be joined there by a Rhodesian air force helicopter to assist with deployment and casevac if needed.

'I will base myself with the Portuguese at Gurue. I'll have Signals Officer Jimmy Munro and a couple of operators with me because I want all ten of you together out in the field. I have told the Colonel we will commit to this operation for two to three weeks. That should be enough time for us to find the Frelimo gang causing the trouble.'

We thanked the Brigadier and headed off to our store, where we perched on ammo boxes to discuss what we'd need to take with us.

'I remember doing a long-term ambush on the Zambezi escarpment with the RLI before I joined the SAS,' I said. 'It was January and as expected it rained solidly. After about ten days we pulled back from the ambush positions to get a resupply.

'Another troop positioned close to us joined us at the resupply point, and one of their boys was in serious trouble. He was shaking and shivering uncontrollably. Our medic went across to see him and said he was suffering from hypothermia. He'd been wet and cold for a protracted period and unless we did something quickly he'd be in even bigger trouble.

'We put him in the front of one of the Land Rovers that brought in the resupply and turned the heater on full. The medic then somehow took off his soaking clothes and got him into dry, warm gear. It took a couple of hours for him to come right.

'We will be getting wet for sure and we don't want anything like that happening. So what do we do, Mack?' I asked. 'You're from Scotland and it's always wet and bloody cold up there. What did you guys do – apart from eating porridge and drinking whisky?'

'Well that would be a good start,' he replied.

'But seriously the porridge suggestion is a good one. It's easy to make and we won't be short of water. A brew and a bowl of porridge would be a great way to start the day. And on top of that, porridge sticks to your ribs.'

We all laughed. We'd never heard that one before.

'Sticks to your ribs?' I asked.

'It means it lasts. You don't feel you need another meal an hour later.'

'Well that sounds good to me,' I replied, and everyone else agreed. We'd get some oats.

'The important thing,' continued Mack, 'is to make sure your sleeping gear and dry clothes, like the camo jacket, stay dry. I can't see it being too much of a problem for us patrolling in our ponchos and getting wet, so long as we can get out of the wet clothes at the end of the day. In Scotland we used 'pack liners' to make sure the critical stuff and our food didn't get wet.

'Basically, a pack liner is just a thick plastic bag, but it has to be well sealed because all through the day it may be sitting in a pool of water in the bottom of your pack.'

'Brilliant, Mack,' I said and turned to Rex.

'What do you reckon, Rex?' I asked. 'Where will we find something like that?'

'Plastic explosive,' Rex replied without a moment's hesitation. 'The 10 kg slabs come in a thick plastic bag that we usually keep. I've seen a pile of them in the magazine. They would be perfect. I'll go down and get some for us once we are done here.'

We opted to take an additional light-weight shelter each we could use as a ground sheet, and cut down on our web belt weight by only taking one water bottle. We took extra brew kit and packet soups, and we found some small packets of beef biltong that were in sealed packaging. The usual game sticks we carried would soon go mouldy in the wet so were not an option.

I opted not to take machine guns, instead choosing to just take our FN rifles, but I boosted our fire power by each of us carrying two 42Z rifle grenades. Fish would have his bazooka, with extra rockets shared out amongst the rest of us.

We each carried four spare magazines for the FN. If we needed more ammunition the Portuguese G3 carbine used the same NATO 7.62mm round so we could get that from them.

Early next day we boarded an air force DC3 for the long flight to Nampula. We flew north-east over the Inyanga Mountains on the border with Mozambique, up to the Zambezi River, across the southern tip of Malawi and on to Nampula.

Looking out of the aircraft window on the final leg between Malawi and Nampula I could see some of the inselbergs the Brigadier had described.

I liked what I was seeing. There was a dense canopy of low woodland, the usual palm trees rising above the figs and hardwoods on the river courses, and around the granite domes the cover was thick and green. Water sparkled in countless streams.

We would have no trouble being invisible in this environment, and we certainly wouldn't have to worry about finding water.

I called Rex over so he too could see our environment.

He shared my enthusiasm: 'Like it, Mick,' he said. 'Can't wait to get on the ground.'

At Nampula we were taken to the Army Headquarters where the Colonel was based. It was a grand building with a marble staircase leading to his office and the operations room where we were given our briefing.

It didn't amount to much.

A Frelimo terrorist gang estimated at twenty to thirty strong had mounted a number of attacks against locals around Gurue. So far the incidents had all been on the northern side of the settlement, suggesting the gang was based somewhere in the massive complex of granite outcrops that extended for many kilometres away to the north.

At least that was a starting point for us.

After the briefing the DC3 took us west to Gurue where we were welcomed by a Portuguese Army Major who was in charge of the local garrison. That afternoon we helped the Brigadier and Jimmy Munro set up their tents and communication systems while we settled into an unused store room.

The helicopter arrived at around 1600 hrs. We were all pleased to see Ian Harvey as the pilot with Butch Grayling his technician. The two of them were a formidable combination. If we got into trouble, they'd find a way of getting us out of it.

The following morning I asked Ian if he could take the Brigadier, Rex and I on a recce flight over the tangled mass of granite features to the north of Gurue.

I explained that apart from giving us a look at the lay of the land, I especially hoped we could find some tracks. I reasoned there must be paths through the area that would be used by local hunters or those looking for honey. Better to get onto one of those tracks than start off by blindly wandering through the bush.

Ian agreed and we took off on what was a beautiful morning in a simply stunning landscape. He tracked along the edge of the bare inselbergs, staying between the thick bush and the open areas of cultivated fields and tea plantations.

We found several tracks. The more promising ones Ian followed into the bush where most ended in small clearings with cultivation – probably marijuana groves.

One looked bigger and better used.

I asked if we could go down and have a look. There was a clearing nearby and Ian put us down. Rex and I jumped out to have a look and we hit gold!

There were tracks with a figure eight pattern. Chinese issue boots. These were terrorist tracks – at least twenty of them.

'Brilliant, Harves, and thank you,' I said as we returned to Gurue.

The helicopter could only take five of us at a time, so while Rex and the first stick headed back to the clearing, I went with the Brigadier to look at the maps. We were looking for clues as to where the track might lead us.

About twenty-five kilometres north of our start point we noticed the granite features spread out somewhat, and formed a circle around a clearing in the centre.

'That would be my guess,' said the Brigadier, and I agreed. It would be a good place to base; far enough away to remain undetected, but centrally located with Portuguese settlements they could target roughly equal distances to the north, south and west.

A fair bit of adrenalin was pumping through my veins as I jumped into the waiting helicopter. I was excited and feeling good. The landscape around us was spectacular, conditions were cool and pleasant for patrolling, and we were on the hunt for a terrorist group. It didn't get much better than this for a soldier.

We adopted our usual formation of Rex up front with Pig Dog Rex keeping his focus on the track and boot prints while Pig Dog scoured the ground ahead looking for movement, listening for sounds and smelling the air.

The rest of us followed a short distance behind keeping our focus on the scouts in front and reacting to any silent signals from them.

We had a break in the middle of the day, then continued our follow-up until just before last light. We moved well away from the track into thick cover where we spent an uneventful first night. Karate sent back our location to the Brigadier. We had covered just over twelve kilometres – roughly half way to our suspected target area.

The following morning dawned bright and sunny. We didn't bother with Mack's porridge – conditions were too good. We made do with a quick brew and a biscuit and were back on the track while the orioles and bulbuls were still singing their wake-up calls.

We made good progress until around 1000 hours when we stopped for another brew and some food. We'd just got packed up when from nowhere there was a big black cloud and it started to rain. We sheltered under some trees while we dug out the ponchos from our packs.

Karate had come up with the good idea of us all getting the biggest size available because that would go some way to also keeping our Bergen backpacks dry.

I went across to Rex.

'This isn't bad news, Rex,' I said. 'My only worry so far on this operation is that our tracks could be followed. Any Frelimo or their couriers using this track couldn't miss the tracks we have made (in spite of us all having specially moulded boot soles with no tread). They wouldn't know who it was, and given the inertia of the Portuguese in their garrison would be unlikely to think it was security forces. Nevertheless, they would be on the lookout for whoever made the tracks.

'If this rain lives up to expectations our tracks will be washed away in an hour or so. This is good for us,' I said.

Rex agreed and added that we should keep walking towards our target area. He thought it was unlikely Frelimo would be out in the rain, and our tracks would be washed out as we went.

'Mick, we should be able to reach the hills that surround that clearing you identified with the Brigadier later this afternoon. In this country we should have no problem finding somewhere to base up in deep cover.

Once we have got ourselves sorted out, we can set up observation points on higher ground and do some local recce work. If there is a camp around there, we'll find it.'

We continued walking along the track in the pouring rain. It was warm enough while we were walking and our ponchos were big enough for us to hold our FNs at the ready underneath them. It wasn't too bad. The odd swirling gust of wind made the ponchos flap around but they worked OK. We weren't bone dry but we certainly weren't going to get hypothermia.

As Rex predicted we reached the huge inselbergs surrounding the clearing. Our hope was that we'd find a sheltered gap where we could safely base up, and hopefully make camp somewhere out of the persistent heavy rain.

We all crouched in cover and the limited shelter of some big trees while Rex and Pig Dog went to look for a camp site.

They returned about an hour later with good news.

Beneath a huge overhanging rock they had found a sheltered area big enough for all of us. It was dry and the deep base of rock hyrax droppings would be very comfortable under our flimsy sleeping bags.

We undid our pack liners that had worked to perfection and took out our dry clothes and sleeping bags. As I snuggled into mine later that evening, I couldn't help but notice a distinct smell of almonds.

'Plastic explosive aromatherapy,' explained Karate. 'Very good for you but don't light a match!'

We had a good night while the rain continued to pour down, and we had Mack's porridge for the first time next morning.

I called the boys together.

'Karate, you and Horse are in charge of looking after our camp while Rex, Pig Dog, Nelson and I go out there in the rain to do some recce work. No point all of us getting soaked at this stage and I'm hoping the weather will keep Frelimo under cover.

'My plan is to keep following the track that has led us here because if there are any bases or staging camps they can't be too far away.

'While we are away send a sitrep to the Brigadier, give him our location, let him know all is OK and that we are doing local recce work. Keep listening on VHF channel five in case we need to contact you, and we'll certainly do that on our way back so you know we are coming.

'I want a guard on high alert keeping watch all the time we are away. Probably a good idea to have the radio with him. We might think we are cute going out in these conditions but we must never underestimate our opposition. They might have the same idea and these Frelimo guys will know this bush better than we do.'

Rex, Nelson, Pig Dog and I got under our ponchos and headed out into the rain.

We found the track but rather than walk on it we kept to one side, about twenty metres away.

If Frelimo were to come down the track we would see or hear them coming. We would drop down out of sight and wait for them to approach. When they were at close range we'd bounce up and open fire at them.

That was our tactic and we advanced ready and waiting for the action.

Nothing happened and we made slow but steady progress between the huge granite masses that surrounded the open area we were interested in.

We eventually found ourselves on the edge of one of the inselbergs, looking out over a flat densely wooded area that extended for about two kilometres in the distance where the gigantic granite features resumed their dominance.

We couldn't see anything except a solid green canopy.

We kept looking.

'Smoke!' said Pig Dog suddenly.

We all sniffed the air and sure enough there was a faint smell of wood smoke.

'Good work, Pig Dog,' I said. 'Let's go and have a closer look.'

We moved cautiously forward, continuing to stay off to one side of the track.

The smoke smell got stronger.

Rex suddenly signalled halt.

We closed in next to him.

He pointed to what looked like the roof of a structure about sixty metres ahead of us.

The cover was still good and the rain was still steady, so we risked going closer.

Hiding behind boulders we had a good look from no more than thirty metres away.

What Rex had spotted was a large open-sided shelter where there was enough room for twenty or more people. We counted ten Frelimo standing or sitting under the shelter. A few carried AKs.

The smoke we had smelled came from a fireplace under cover inside the shelter. Frelimo would use it for cooking and warmth in this cool and very wet place.

Beyond the shelter we counted twelve thatched bivvies – the usual 'A' frame design we knew so well.

We backed off. We'd seen enough.

This was a staging base and the Frelimo here would be a caretaker group who would also participate in the various raids they had made against Gurue. Staging bases also typically had arms caches, often built up in preparation for a major attack. We'd have a good look once we'd dealt with the incumbents.

While we trudged back to our overhang in the rain, I was thinking about how best to attack this base, and as usual I was greedy – I wanted all of them. I could live with one or two escaping our attack, but no more.

When we were close, we used the VHF radio to let Karate know we were coming in.

First priority was to get out of our wet clothes and make some hot tea.

Everyone gathered round as I sipped the brew and thawed out my hands with the warmth of the aluminium billy.

I explained what we had found and made a crude model using stones and sticks to give the others an idea of the Frelimo camp layout.

'Here's what are we going to do about it,' I said, and everyone looked on expectantly.

'You have all been with me long enough to know that now and then I come up with something different, and tonight that is the case.'

They looked at me with increased interest, but bemusement at the same time, wondering what the hell I'd come up with.

Horse did his usual. 'Don't worry, boys. We all know the Major. It will be nothing more than business as usual. Submarine attacks, night bombing, the madness of cutting away from freefall parachutes. All business as usual. This won't be any different!' and his infectious laughter and light hearted taking the piss out of me got everyone going and relaxed.

I'd never tell him but I really appreciated his interjections because it got us together and made everyone listen with interest. He was a terrific guy to have in a team.

'We are going to use this persistent bloody rain to our advantage' I said.

'Whoever is on guard at 0100 hours is to wake everybody up at 0200 at the end of that stag. We should all make a brew and some of Mack's porridge – there is plenty of time.

'We will leave the packs here and just carry our web belts and rifles under the poncho.

'Rex, can you get things underway by taking a compass bearing from here to the track. I know it isn't far away but at 0230 hours in the dark and rain I want to be sure we find it. I guess we should mount the night scope on your rifle, that will also help with finding our way and we'll need it at the camp anyway.

'We'll follow Rex from here to the track, and once we have found it we'll follow it into the Frelimo base camp.

'When we get to the camp Rex will use the scope to see if there is a guard in the shelter, or maybe somebody sleeping there in front of the fire. If there is, then Rex that's your target, but my guess is that in this miserable weather they will all be tucked up in the shelter of the bivvies, and at around 0330 hours in the morning will be fast asleep.

'That being the case we will silently walk through the camp and I'll position one of you on the left side of each bivvie so we will all be shooting in the same direction. There are twelve bivvies but only ten of us so at the top end of the camp Karate and Pig Dog will each have two bivvies to take care of. They are close together so I don't see that being too much of an issue.

'Once I've positioned you next to your bivvie, take off the safety catch, put it on the automatic setting and be ready to fire.

'I'll get things started by opening fire when I see Karate and Pig Dog in place.

'When you hear my firing, you are to empty the magazine into the bivvie, spraying the fire around so you don't miss anything inside.

'Karate, you and Pig Dog have two bivvies, so use half a magazine on each.

'Once we have used the first magazine, change quickly and listen for noise inside the bivvies.

'If you hear anything give it another burst. We're not taking prisoners.

'Once I've judged we have done as much damage as we can I'll shout out "Make Safe" and then we'll all go back to their shelter. There is plenty of room for all of us and we'll be out of the rain. We'll stay there until first light then we'll have a look at what we have done. I'm also pretty certain a base like this will have a cache that shouldn't be too far away. It would be good to find it.

'If Rex finds a guard at the shelter, we'll leave him and Jonny to take care of that while the rest of us go around behind and move into the camp from the other end.

'The only other scenario I can think of is if we are seen as we move into the camp and they shout out a warning. If that happens, we will all charge through the camp shooting into the bivvies as we go.

'Can't think of anything else. What do you think?' I asked.

'Bloody brilliant,' said Pig Dog and there were nods of agreement all round.

'Thank you,' I said. 'Once we are finished at the Frelimo camp we'll head back to this base and let the Brigadier know what we've been up to. They won't be flying in this sort of weather, but if it clears up he will want to come in for a look and probably bring some Portuguese at the same time. We'll see what the weather does and decide then what we want to do, but right now I'm in no hurry to leave this cavern.'

Everyone agreed with that as well – it was very comfortable and a great place for us.

With the wind and driving rain just metres away from us outside the overhanging rock, everybody was early into our almond flavoured sleeping bags. We had a big night ahead of us, and it would be out in that wind and driving rain.

Jonny shook us all awake at 0200 and we lit up our small gas stoves to get water on the boil. It wasn't often we could do this before a camp attack, but hidden in our cavern there was no risk of compromise.

Just before moving off I called everyone together for a final briefing.

'Rex and I will go in front, and Karate you and Pig Dog bring up the rear as you'll be the last to be deployed at the camp. Doesn't matter what order the rest of you take in between.

'I had one more thought about the attack. I think there are a couple of bivvies that are very much in line and I don't want us shooting at each other. Where I see that is a risk, I'll put two of you together: one to deal with the nearest bivvie while the second person takes on the one further away. The second bivvie may be ten metres away or more, so instead of firing on automatic better to use up the magazine with a series of double taps.'

As we followed Rex towards the track, I noticed the rain had eased up somewhat, but now there was a strong wind. I was happy with that. It made the forest noisy. Nobody would hear us as we moved into position.

We reached the edge of the camp.

Rex signalled a halt and we all dropped down while he checked out the shelter with the night scope.

Rex turned to me.

'All clear,' he whispered. 'Let's go!'

I positioned Rex next to the first bivvie then we crept through the camp. I only had to double up once. I put Horse and Jonny together where two bivvies were in line with each other.

The rest of us stood within two metres of each bivvie.

As I watched Pig Dog and Karate move into position and wave OK to me, I opened fire into the bivvie next to me. I fired on automatic but used up the magazine in three decent bursts making sure no corner of the flimsy grass shelter was missed.

The noise of the gunfire stopped as abruptly as it had started.

We all changed magazines and listened for any sounds coming from the bivvies.

Horse opened fire again with a series of double taps. I had a small smile to myself, knowing he'd be wishing he had the machine gun he normally carried. There would be no sounds if he'd used that!

We waited another five minutes, then satisfied with the situation I called out 'Make Safe' and put on my safety catch.

We wandered back through the camp and made our way to the shelter where we made ourselves as comfortable as we could and waited for first light.

It was a gloomy daybreak. The rain had eased to a light drizzle but the thick cloud came as low as the tree canopy.

'We'll each check our bivvies,' I said.

'If there is a body inside pull it out clear of the entrance and leave it there. Check inside the bivvies for packs and weapons. Collect whatever there is of interest and bring it back to this shelter.'

When we had finished half an hour later there were eleven bodies stretched out next to the bivvies. One of Pig Dog's two bivvies at the top end of the camp was the only unoccupied structure.

And we had eleven packs lined up in the shelter along with nine AKs and two older SKS carbines.

The rain had intensified again so I told everyone we'd call it quits for the day and return to the comfort of our cavern. I didn't see much sense in looking for an arms cache in the pouring rain when all the terrorists were dead anyway. It could wait.

Back at our cavern and in dry clothes my priority with Karate was to get a message back to the Brigadier, while Rex had everyone else cleaning and lightly oiling the FN rifles.

We told the Brigadier we were currently enveloped in thick cloud but the wind had come up again and it might clear away the weather later in the day. We told him there was an LZ for the helicopter in a small clearing close to our cavern, and asked if he'd bring the fully charged batteries we'd left at Gurue for the HF radio and the night scope. We'd give him our used ones to take back and put on charge. I also asked for 200 rounds of ammunition and another two days' ration packs.

With that resupply we'd be good for another week or so because we weren't stopping here. It was our belief the track that led us to this first camp was a Frelimo Ho Chi Minh Trail. There would be other camps along it.

We'd keep following the track and we'd find and destroy them. One after the other.

Frelimo didn't know who we were. We'd do our best to remain invisible and keep it that way. On top of that the lack of military effort from the Portuguese had perhaps lulled them into a false sense of security. Buoyed by the success of our night raid I was confident we were on top here, and we all wanted more.

The cloud cleared early in the afternoon. The trees still dripped water but there was blue sky and it was warmer.

We guided in Ian Harvey and the Brigadier with the radio and marked his LZ with orange smoke as he closed in. The Portuguese Major had tagged along with another man in plain clothes I guessed was DGS Police.

I left four of the boys with the helicopter while the rest of us walked to the camp – about twenty minutes away.

'OK Mick,' said the Brigadier as we reached the shelter. 'Take us through what happened step by step. We didn't even know you were onto a camp. What happened?'

I explained how we had done a late afternoon recce in the rain the previous day and how we found the camp. I went on to say that I thought we should take advantage of the conditions because I believed the Frelimo terrorists would be doing what any sensible human would be doing at 3.30 in the morning in such cold wet weather. They'd be tucked up in the warmth of a blanket inside their shelters.

We didn't play by the normal rules, and I was totally confident we could walk into the camp that night without any fear of detection.

I then walked to the nearest shelter to show them where we positioned ourselves, and explained how we each emptied a twenty-round magazine on automatic into the flimsy structures.

'*Incrível! Inacreditável!*' exclaimed the Portuguese Major. Incredible.

We were appreciative of his compliment.

We sat inside the shelter while the DGS man got to work on the packs and weapons we had pulled out of the bivvies. Rex meanwhile split our group and commenced a sweep around the camp. We were sure there would be a cache hidden somewhere and were keen to find it.

'In all my years in the army I've never heard of anything as brazen as this, and what a great result. Eleven dead Frelimo. 100 per cent kill. That doesn't happen often,' said the Brigadier.

'It's a great start to the operation. Colonel Costa Da Silva will be delighted. So, what's next, Mick?' he asked.

'Sir, we think this is a major highway and there will be more camps along the way. If we keep following the trail, we'll find them, and we'll take them out. One after the other.

'Relentless pursuit. It won't be something Frelimo have experienced before and they won't like it.'

'I certainly do,' replied the Brigadier.

'We'll dry things out here tonight and enjoy the fresh rations you brought in for us, then if it's OK with you and Harves, I wouldn't mind being uplifted first thing in the morning and dropped off somewhere suitable about fifteen kilometres ahead. As a general rule we reckon they build their camps a day's walking apart, which for Frelimo will be around twenty-five kilometres, so we won't be too close and it will save us time.

'Makes sense. No problem,' he replied.

And at that point a beaming Rex arrived with the boys all carrying boxes of the 7.62mm Intermediate ammunition the communist bloc used, as well as a couple of TMH46 landmines.

They had found a small trail, but Rex, the master tracker, had no trouble following it to some scattered boulders. In a sheltered and dry position beneath one of the larger boulders they found the cache.

And that topped off what had been a pretty good day for us.

The next morning was beautiful but cloud had settled into the lower valleys and Harves couldn't fly until the sun had burned it off.

We all made porridge while we waited.

Mack got us to try it with a sprinkling of salt on top. Most of us preferred it sweet but it wasn't bad and medic man Fish pointed out that a bit of extra salt before a day when we'd sweat a lot wouldn't be a bad thing.

Harves eventually arrived and took us in two lifts across a densely wooded area to the edge of another cluster of the incredible inselbergs.

The track we were following was as prominent as ever – in fact if anything it was getting a bit wider. The rain had washed away any prints but we pushed on at a steady pace, ready to react if a Frelimo patrol approached.

And it didn't matter to us if any such patrol consisted of just three or three hundred terrorists. There were only ten of us but they wouldn't know that, and through aggressive action we'd make sure they wouldn't find out. We'd make them think they were up against a hundred.

Late afternoon as we were thinking about basing up for the night Rex signalled an urgent halt.

I carefully moved up next to him.

'Bivvies, Mick,' he said, and pointed them out twenty or thirty metres ahead.

'Good job, Rex. We'll sit tight for a few minutes to look and listen.'

It was very quiet and we soon realised there were no terrorists in what turned out to be a small camp consisting of just six of the usual A-frame thatched bivvies.

We checked them all without finding anything of interest, then moved on leaving them intact. They were too green to burn and I didn't want to advertise our presence.

The following day the track twisted through another cluster of huge inselbergs. Soldiers don't like patrolling through narrow spaces surrounded by high ground, but we had no such fear in this environment. The granite islands were very steep, in some cases almost vertical, impossible for humans to climb. They were the domain of eagles and rock hyraxes, whose gecko-like feet enabled them clamber up the rock and into their shelters amongst cracks and chasms.

Late that afternoon we reached the edge of the inselberg plain. Ahead of us the country was flat and well wooded. To the north, maybe twenty kilometres away, we could see the bare peaks of more granite.

We stopped to look at the maps and work out exactly where we were.

Directly ahead of us and close was the small settlement of Cuamba. I didn't want to be seen by locals but Rex and I were both puzzled by not seeing any footprints on our track that clearly led to Cuamba. We decided to go and have a look.

There was good woodland cover right to the edge of the village where we could see several thatched mud huts, but the place was deserted. The only life we saw were two very thin dogs.

'This is Frelimo at work,' I said. 'They have rounded up all the locals and will have taken them away to one of their camps.'

We walked through the deserted village.

A flock of black and white crows suddenly took flight in alarm, startling us.

We went to investigate and found the bodies of two African males lying on the ground. Their shirts had been taken off and we could see multiple wounds from bayonets and bullets in their bare backs.

'Frelimo,' I said again. 'These two may have shown dissent, but most likely they were local elders. Samora Machel has decreed that all local chiefs and headmen must be eliminated.

'How long do you think they have they been dead, Rex?' I asked.

The bodies had been further mutilated by the crows and probably other animals but Rex estimated they were killed no more than three or four days previously.

We moved away from the stench and it wasn't long before the crows started to return.

I decided to move back into the bush on the south side of the settlement and make camp for the night.

Karate rigged up the radio and we sent our location and a report to the Brigadier. We said we believed another Frelimo camp was about twenty kilometres away in the next granite cluster to the north. We asked for the helicopter to leapfrog us along the track as before and let them know there was plenty of space for the aircraft to land next to the settlement of Cuamba. Good landing zones for the helicopter were not easy to find in this thickly wooded country.

The other good news was that the weather continued to be fine as Harves picked up my stick next morning and took us forward on the track.

'Dunno where we are going to put you down, Mick,' said Harves over the headsets as we looked down on a solid green canopy.

We kept flying for another five minutes when Harves suddenly turned the aircraft to his right. He'd spotted a clearing. It was tight but he'd get us in OK.

The helicopter hovered about six feet off the ground and we all jumped out. We crouched down as the Alouette powered up to lift out of the clearing and returned to bring Rex.

The five of us fanned out and moved away from the LZ when suddenly there was a scream and an African woman ran away from us.

We jogged forward and there were more civilians.

We'd been dropped next to a camp.

Knowing Frelimo put the civilians on the outside of their camps we continued jogging forward past their thatched bivvies, looking for targets, but ignoring the increasing number of women and children running around us.

We'd got maybe twenty metres in towards the centre of the camp when suddenly the ground next to my right foot was stitched by RPD machine gun fire.

I dived to the ground and rolled away to my left, and I kept rolling as the machine gun fire followed my progress. I reached two good sized trees that would be good cover and had a look at what was happening.

I wondered why I hadn't heard firing from the boys, but as I looked I could see dozens of women and children running in front of us. Between us and the terrorist with the RPD.

We couldn't return fire for fear of hitting these panicking civilians, but that didn't stop the guy with the machine gun.

I watched in disbelief as he gunned down first one then a second woman running across his line of fire.

A burst erupted at the base of my tree; bark flying everywhere.

What could we do?

How could we defend ourselves with all these civilians running in front of us?

I looked up again, hoping for an opportunity to return fire, but to my horror a very elderly woman started hobbling across our front.

'No!' I shouted. 'Go back!'

She may have heard me but she wouldn't have understood.

I saw the RPD gunner adjust his aim and I swear he deliberately aimed at the old woman who collapsed on the ground as the bullets ripped through her.

It was a cruel callous act, but he'd never do anything like it again.

As he fired at the old lady, Fish suddenly had clear air.

I heard the *Whoosh* of his bazooka then watched with satisfaction as it blew away the terrorist and his machine gun.

Next priority was to get on the VHF radio to let Harves know we were in contact in a camp.

'Drop Rex off in the same place, Harves, then head north. Butch may get targets on the track leading out of here, but be warned there are heaps of civilians.'

Harves acknowledged, Rex was dropped off and joined us, and then the Alouette went hunting.

Harves increased the height and went into an anti-clockwise orbit, giving Butch with his 7.62mm GPMG a clear view of the ground below.

The helicopter opened fire.

Frelimo were now also being pursued from the air.

Relentless pursuit as Butch gunned them down.

We meanwhile had spread out and were slowly advancing through the camp.

There were more than one hundred civilians who sat fearfully together in groups as we moved past them and into the terrorist camp proper.

There was a shelter similar to the one at our first camp and forty thatched bivvies. Nobody had stuck around to see who we were, and they'd left in a big hurry, leaving many weapons and backpacks behind.

In one pack I found a copy of Mao's *Little Red Book*. I wondered if there was a Chinese commissar attached to this group but could find nothing more to suggest that was the case.

We advanced along the track to the north of the camp.

There were many boot prints – more than fifty, Rex estimated.

Harves guided us to where they fired at the fleeing Frelimo.

We found five bodies on the track, and another four in different locations further on.

There were still a lot of Frelimo at large, but we'd not finished with them.

We'd keep following, and every time we met there would be a few less.

Harves meanwhile needed to return to base to refuel, so we went back into the camp.

I asked Nelson to speak to the locals.

We told them they would not be harmed and were now free of the Frelimo who treated them as slaves. They told us they had been rounded up at Cuamba and forced to make camp with Frelimo. They said there was very little food, and what they could find had to go to Frelimo.

We told them they could not at the moment return to Cuamba – they were not safe there. Instead they would be resettled at Gurue where the Portuguese had built a protected village. Nelson said that one day when the fighting stopped, they would be allowed to go back to their homes at Cuamba.

We all dug into our packs and gave them some food while we waited for the Brigadier to arrive with the usual contingent of Portuguese who would be keen to see the camp.

While we were waiting Rex and I dug out the maps and had a look at where the track to the north might go, and where our next confrontation with Frelimo may be.

It didn't really give us any useful clues.

Not far ahead of us and to the east was another inselberg block, but beyond that the country was less featured and there were no marked local settlements until one reached Micuna which was over one hundred kilometres north of us.

The problem was we were getting further and further away from Gurue. It meant the helicopter took more time and fuel to reach us, and when it did it had limited flying time to help us.

But they had nowhere else to go.

Gurue was the only base the Portuguese had in the area.

We explained all this to the Brigadier, suggesting we continue following the Frelimo tracks for another day. We'd see what happened and make a call thereafter.

The Portuguese meanwhile led the locals back to their village at Cuamba. There was a rough track leading to it that a truck could use. They'd pick them up and take them to the protected village at Gurue – the *aldeamento* as the Portuguese called such settlements.

The following day we kept going and soon reached the inselberg block that was as spectacular as ever. There were many Frelimo boot prints on the track that to our surprise suddenly swung east around the granite block.

We kept going. The compass said we were heading just south of due east, and the track didn't deviate from that bearing for the next two hours.

Rex and I again checked the map. We were heading towards the two settlements of Mutueli and Muirassa, about thirty kilometres away, and it looked very promising.

They were situated in a remarkable looking area, with massive inselbergs arranged in a circular formation, not unlike a crater. It would be good country for Frelimo.

Good too for the helicopter, because with every step we moved slightly closer to Gurue.

We let the Brigadier know, then Rex pushed the pace until it got dark.

The morning dawned cold and cloudy and the wind had got up. It was going to rain again.

After a brew and some porridge we were back on the track that was still heading east-south-east. In the distance we could see some gigantic features with jagged tops that promised to be even more spectacular than anything we'd seen so far. Surely this would be where we'd find Frelimo?

We stopped for a brew mid-morning and took out our ponchos. The rain wasn't far away.

The map showed two clusters of inselbergs running parallel with each other and about a kilometre apart. Where we were heading, another ten kilometres further away, the two lines of granite curved in towards each other and made a circle. On the map it looked just like a massive volcanic crater. Most of these inselbergs were just under three thousand feet high, with a few peaking at just over that.

We weren't unhappy when it started to rain.

Our ponchos worked well, our tracks were being washed out and I was sure Frelimo would believe they could safely relax in their camp shelters. The Portuguese had given them no reason to think otherwise. They had never been followed by Portuguese troops.

The last camp encounter would be regarded as a chance happening, probably caused by a traitor from the village of Cuamba.

They didn't know we were coming.

I was determined they would find out the hard way.

But first we had to find them.

We pressed on in the rain until late afternoon when I called a halt at the base of one of the big granite mounds. We took shelter under trees while Rex and Pig Dog went looking for a suitable camp site. We were all hoping they'd find another big dry cavern like our first base in the rain.

And what they found wasn't at all bad.

They led us to a narrow crack between two towering granite piers. We could see a narrow line of light way above us. The rain dripped down on the rock wall facing the wind but the other wall was dry, and against this wall was a dry strip a metre and a half wide.

'There is room for everyone in this dry strip if we spread out in a long line,' said Rex.

'I don't think Frelimo will be out tonight but, Mick, we should put a guard out now just in case we are wrong.'

I agreed. I put my pack down in what would be my sleeping space and took the first guard. I wanted to look at the maps and think about things while the boys got dry and made themselves comfortable.

About twenty minutes later Rex joined me with two billies of hot tea.

'What are you thinking, Mick?' he asked as I took a sip of the welcome brew.

'It's the usual problem we have when a small group like ours is on the heels of a much bigger force,' I replied. 'No matter how much we take them by surprise our numbers limit the amount of damage we can do.'

Psychologically I really struggled to accept that. We put so much time and effort into tracking down these terrorist groups my brain just demanded more than a handful of kills.

'Geez Rex, we walk day and night in the pouring bloody rain. We go to great lengths to stay invisible, and we take pride in our all-round skills as soldiers. We deserve the maximum return.'

'Well, we've had it a good few times as I recall,' Rex replied, 'but night bombing by Canberras isn't an option up here in this weather and with these bloody huge mountains. We'll have to think of something different.'

'Yes. You're right, and this time the Brigadier won't be able to pull mortars out of his hat like he did for us in Angola.'

'So, it's the ten of us and a helicopter against what the tracks tell us will be forty to fifty Frelimo in a camp that I'm sure isn't too far away,' said Rex. 'How do we make the most of what we've got?'

'We've also got the weather,' I replied. 'If it's hosing down it gives us the chance of getting close-up amongst them again as we did in that first camp attack. That would improve our chances of getting a bigger kill. But we then get nothing extra from the helicopter.

'And if it's good weather there are problems using the helicopter as an airborne assault unit if there is an attached civilian camp like at the last place.

'If there is a civilian camp we will have to think of a way to take it out of play,' I added, 'but first we have to find the camp and then we can look again at the alternatives.'

We finished our tea and I thanked Rex. I enjoyed these discussions with him and we did it a lot.

I'd heard there were relationship issues in 22 SAS with officers being disparagingly referred to as 'Rupert' by NCOs and the men.

No such problems in C Squadron, but then we in Rhodesia didn't have royalty and a lingering class system that was probably responsible for such taunts. Either way it's not an ideal situation for any elite Special Forces unit that operates in small groups and I hope the commanders fixed it.

The following day it was still raining and we were back in our ponchos and on the track that was still heading east.

We found ourselves in a flat well-wooded area with towering inselbergs on both sides of us. Not that we could see the tops as the cloud and rain swirled through gaps on both sides and sat just a few feet above the tree canopy where we walked.

I made the call for us to stay on the track, and to stay close together because I didn't believe that in these weather conditions we were in any danger of being ambushed by Frelimo. We nevertheless advanced with caution and everyone was on high alert, knowing that if we did meet a Frelimo patrol we'd have to react very quickly.

The rain intensified mid-morning, and what started out as a light showering suddenly became a deluge with strong swirling winds.

Our ponchos could handle the light stuff but this was in another league and soon we were all soaking wet.

'Rex,' I said, 'there are no prizes for being out in this stuff. Let's find somewhere we can shelter while this front does its thing. Frelimo will still be here when it's over.'

Rex led us off the track and headed for the nearest inselberg that wasn't too far away. These amazing features had given us shelter before and our best option was to try them again.

We struggled through some thick vines at the base of a feature and eventually found a narrow game track, probably made by rock hyraxes.

Suddenly the vegetation cleared and we were at the entrance to a cave.

As we moved forward there were four African men and a boy huddled around a small fire.

Rex and I stood in front of them with our rifles in the aim.

'Don't move!' I shouted and gestured they should keep down on their haunches.

Rex and I both scanned the cave and couldn't see any weapons.

'Nelson!' I shouted. 'I need you up here with us now!'

He arrived a moment later, and seeing the situation immediately went forward and stood in front of the four men spread out around the fire.

'If you are Frelimo,' he started in their language, 'your lives are in great danger because Frelimo are our enemy and we are here to kill them.

'Who are you?' he demanded. 'Tell us why we shouldn't kill you.'

The older looking of the four men turned to Nelson and said, 'There is no reason to kill us. Frelimo are our enemy as well.

'I am Mlando, headman of the village known as Muirassa, and this man,' he said pointing to one of the others, 'is Surezi, the headman of Mutueli village. We are neighbours.

'Two months ago, a Frelimo gang arrived at Muirassa demanding to know who was the headman and telling the people they were being taken away to become part of the Frelimo campaign against the Portuguese.

'One of the older women stood up to them and said they would give them food but would not be leaving their village.

'In front of everyone she was gunned down by the Frelimo cadres. They were youths and young. They would know nothing but they had the AK47s so they could do whatever they wanted.

'A young girl was grabbed by two of them and it became obvious what their intention was. Her mother rushed forward to protect her daughter but was gunned down.

'While this was happening one of the young boys – Elijah,' and he pointed to the lad sitting with them, 'slipped away and ran to warn us. My two brothers and I were in the forest at the time collecting poles for some new huts we were planning to build when he arrived.

'We had heard about Frelimo and their communist idea of killing all chiefs and headmen. We had no guns to defend ourselves so we crept close to the village to observe what was happening.

'The people were all rounded up and sat on the ground in the centre of the village, while the Frelimo gang looted the huts. In my wife's hut they found a transistor radio. They asked who it belonged to. My wife said it was hers and was immediately shot while still holding our two young children in her arms.

'The people were ordered to gather what personal possessions they could carry and were led away to make a camp next to the Frelimo base deep in the bush.'

Nelson translated all this and I quickly realised these men were no threat to us.

Just the opposite in fact and it might be a telling factor in our future plans.

The rest of the team meanwhile had moved in to take shelter in what was a large cave. Plenty of room for all of us.

Nelson told the men and the boy to relax.

He complimented the boy on what he had done and said we'd bring them some food and listen to the rest of their story.

We were all happy to be out of the driving rain and meeting these four men and the boy had put a new twist on our operation.

I wasn't unhappy about it, and said so to Rex.

'Normally the last thing we would want is to be compromised by locals, but this is different. These guys have a serious and justified grudge against Frelimo and they want to be rid of them. I'm sure they will help us as much as they can because they want their families and homes back.

'And my guess is that now we won't have to worry about finding Frelimo because these guys will know where they are. They can take us to them.'

Once everyone was sorted out and comfortable, we collected five billies and boiled up 'hearty beef' soup from the packets we carried. We took them to our new comrades. The soup was hot and nutritious, and as they sipped it they told Nelson they had been living on water and a few green bananas. This was the first proper food they'd had in three days.

We let them finish the soup then Nelson asked Mlando to continue with his story.

'Frelimo took our people away into the hills, but a few weeks later they turned up at the village of Mutueli. Surezi was lucky like us to be away looking for beehives when they arrived, because much the same happened there. A few people were shot then the rest were led away to the same camp with the people from Muirassa.

'Surezi came looking for us at Muirassa. We told him what had happened at our village and we have all been looking for our people ever since.'

'And have you found them?' Nelson quickly asked.

'Yes,' he said. 'They are in a camp where the mountains make a circle. It is not far from here.'

We gave each of them one of the spare light-weight shelters we were carrying. They weren't very warm but would be an insulating layer that would give them more comfort than what they'd had for the last few weeks.

We had a guard through the night keeping an eye on things but there were no issues and I slept soundly, confident we'd made some new and useful friends.

For the third day in a row the rain continued and that was OK because I wanted Mlando to show us the Frelimo camp.

I left Karate in charge at the cave, while Nelson joined Rex and I on the recce with Mlando.

I had a sudden idea and asked Nelson to let the young Elijah know he was coming with us. We put a poncho over him then tied it up around his shoulders so it didn't drag on the ground.

Nelson explained to Mlando that Rex and I would lead just in case we encountered Frelimo. He and Elijah would stay with him and show us where to go.

He took us back on the track we had been following. We stayed on it for just over an hour and by that time we were much closer to what we could see of the inselbergs on both sides of us.

Mlando indicated we should leave the track. We sat down for a break and he explained that soon the hills on both sides would curve in together, making a circle, and it was in that feature that Frelimo had made their camp.

Mlando then led the way with Nelson. He was cautious as we advanced. The rain had eased up slightly but it was gloomy and visibility remained limited.

He was good and Rex and I liked what we were seeing.

Now and then he'd stop to scan the ground ahead. He'd point and whisper something to Nelson. Nelson would nod and we'd all follow to his next staging point.

We reached a cluster of boulders where he stopped us.

We all crouched down around him.

'We are at the camp,' he said.

'Just twenty metres from here are the first shelters. These are where our people live. They have now built more than twenty of them. Fifty metres beyond these shelters is the Frelimo camp. They have many shelters including one big one in the middle which is their kitchen. When we came here before we saw ten of them with AKs sitting around there.'

I asked if there were any other tracks, apart from the one we had been following, that led in and out of the camp.

Mlando explained there were two gaps in the encircling hills behind the camp, and there were tracks through these that led to his village. They had followed these to find the camp in the first place, but continued further into the hills where there were more places to hide.

'Nelson, please explain to Mlando that tomorrow morning just as it gets light, we are going to attack Frelimo and free his people. But for them to be safe they must stay inside their shelters. If they come out, they may be killed or injured in the action and we don't want that.'

Nelson translated and Mlando replied at length.

'He says he will go into the camp and tell them,' said Nelson.

'Good. Thank you Mlando, that is what I had hoped for, but you should only risk going to the huts closest to us here. If you go further and are seen by Frelimo you may be shot or captured and that may compromise our operation.

'But a young boy like Elijah running from one hut to another would not arouse any suspicion as there are probably several young children here in this camp. He could spread the word where you could not?' I suggested.

Nelson translated and Elijah bobbed his head in agreement, excited at the prospect of helping us.

Mlando spoke to Elijah at length and then the two of them crept forward towards the flimsy thatched shelters.

'I don't think there will be any problem,' I said to Rex and Nelson as they disappeared into the gloom, 'but I think we should take some basic precautions.'

I looked around and about sixty metres away spotted another cluster of boulders.

'We'll wait over there,' I said, and took a 42Z grenade from my belt. After loading the ballistite cartridge, I fitted it snuggly over the launcher at the end of the FN barrel.

'If there are any surprises, we will be ready for them.'

Rex and Nelson followed suit as we settled into our new location, at the ready, waiting for Mlando and Elijah to return.

We waited for one of the longest hours I have ever experienced, then finally the two of them appeared back where we started, looking around for us. Nelson went forward; they saw him and came hastily to join us.

'All OK?' Nelson asked.

Mlando smiled and said, 'Yes. Everybody knows. They will stay inside the shelters tomorrow until we tell them to come out.'

Nelson gave me the thumbs up and we lost no time in getting away from the Frelimo camp and onto the track that would take us back to our cave.

There was still a possibility we might run into a Frelimo patrol on the track, so in spite of our impatience to get out of the rain, I insisted we take the usual precautions.

We had no intention of being compromised on the eve of another camp attack. As usual my plan hinged on us having the advantage of surprise. If a patrol came along, we'd hide and let them go, happy for them to be casualties the following morning.

Nobody did come along the track and the rain continued to obscure our footprints that were now confused with Elijah's small barefoot print and Mlando's car tyre sandals.

That afternoon we let the Brigadier know what we had found and what we were going to do about it, and the good news was the rain was abating. There were small patches of blue sky appearing suggesting that the next day would be clear.

We hoped so because we had asked Ian Harvey to join us as an airborne stop group. We would oust Frelimo from their camp and those who we didn't reach we reckoned would head for the two gaps in the hills Mlando had told us about.

We wanted Ian and Butch with his GPMG to cover these escape routes, and with all the civilians safely staying inside their shelters anyone spotted from above could only be Frelimo.

The Brigadier acknowledged and we set about organising ourselves for the attack in the morning.

The guard shook us all awake at 0300 and the boys got the billies going to make tea and porridge. I wandered outside the cave to check on the weather. I couldn't see much but it wasn't raining.

Half an hour later we were on the move, following the track towards the Frelimo camp. We had left our packs in the cave and were not encumbered by ponchos, so the going was easy and quiet. The sky above us was clear and star-filled.

Mlando guided us into the same clump of boulders we'd hidden behind yesterday, and here we paused. It was now 0437 hours. We needed to be in position next to the Frelimo shelters in the next ten minutes.

I wanted to leave the attack as late as I could to give Ian Harvey time to reach us in the helicopter, but if Frelimo got up early, we wouldn't wait.

Mlando, his two brothers, Surezi and Elijah went forward and we watched them entering some of the shelters housing their people. They would reassure them and hopefully keep them inside.

We meanwhile silently crept towards the Frelimo shelters. I'd organised the boys into pairs and we spread ourselves out along the edge of the bivvies – no more than five metres away from them.

We crouched down and waited.

At 0510 a few birds had started to twitter, but it was still pitch dark.

I'd give it another five minutes.

It took an eternity, but still there was no movement from any of the bivvies.

'OK let's go!' I shouted and fired a burst into the nearest shelter.

Nelson, my partner in the attack, did the same to another closer to him.

We both then ran forward to engage the next two or three shelters ahead of us.

And that was my tactic.

I argued that Frelimo, with sleep still in their eyes, would have no answer to ten rampant SAS men running through their camp, shooting into the shelters and at any human target that presented itself. And there were a few of those as our rapid assault reached the far end of the camp. Some went down but some escaped.

They wouldn't get far because Ian Harvey and Butch had arrived.

I lobbed out a smoke grenade to show where we were, then moments later we heard firing from the aircraft. Butch had already found targets.

The helicopter orbited and there was more gunfire.

On the ground meanwhile we regrouped and started a slow careful sweep back through the camp.

We hadn't gone far when an AK opened up from one of the bivvies.

Bullets whizzed through the air above our heads.

Nelson and I dropped into a crouch and emptied our magazines into the shelter. The shooting stopped.

We continued our sweep, carefully checking each shelter. As we progressed through the camp there were several shelters that were empty. The Frelimo who escaped from these were lucky but were not necessarily out of the woods. Pursuit would continue from the air and if they were seen they were dead.

By the time we reached our start point we'd counted twenty-seven bodies, and I checked in with Harves in the chopper.

'We've nailed a few, Mick,' he replied to my question, 'but several made it to the narrow gaps between the hills. We checked the opposite side but nobody came through, so they are holed up in cover waiting for us to go away.

'It would be tricky for you guys to winkle them out. There is a lot of cover behind boulders and big lumps of rock. It would be easy to take casualties,' he added.

'Thanks, Ian,' I replied. 'We might be able to get them out for you. Can you orbit above where you think they are to give us an indication, then give me five minutes to get organised?'

'No problem, Mick,' and he banked the aircraft in the direction of one of the huge inselbergs. He then went into a tight orbit.

'Just below us, Mick. That OK?'

'Perfect. We'll let you know when we're ready.'

Reaching into my own webbing I turned to the team. '42Zs,' I said. 'Dig them out. We'll use them like mortars. We'll fire them into the gap. With all the rock in there the shrapnel should fly everywhere. It may well get Frelimo on the move again.'

Apart from Fish who carried the bazooka we were each carrying two of the rifle grenades, so we had eighteen in all to use on Frelimo.

The grenades fit tightly over the launcher at the end of the FN barrel. They are propelled by a 'ballistite' cartridge, which is like a big blank.

Usually the grenades are fired at low trajectory from the shoulder, and this is very accurate, but if the butt of the FN is placed on the ground and the rifle barrel angled at 45° the grenade flies like a mortar with a range of 800 metres.

I got Horse and Jonny to unload a magazine with live rounds and replace them with the ballistite cartridges for the grenades.

I put them five metres apart, and then while holding their rifle butts firmly on the ground, Rex and I angled the barrels and lined them up with the gap in the hills.

We stood behind them to ensure they kept the aim, while Karate and Pig Dog fitted the grenades to the end of the barrels. They then carefully removed the small red safety pins.

Rex and I checked the aim and angle of the barrels again.

'Fire!' I shouted.

As the two grenades soared into the sky, Karate and Pig Dog fitted another two to the rifles. Rex and I checked the alignment and angles, and we fired again.

Another two grenades flew towards Frelimo.

While this was going on Fish had briefed Harves in the chopper and he took up an orbit position a safe distance away on the opposite side of the gap.

Frelimo now had two choices.

They could stay in the gap and be bombed by our grenades, or they could run through to the opposite side and into the waiting gun of the helicopter.

Our eighteen grenades peppered the gap. They made a lot of noise and black smoke on exploding. We checked later and can't claim to have inflicted casualties, but that didn't matter because they got Frelimo on the run.

Harves spotted a gang of twelve running along a track.

He turned the aircraft sharply in their direction and the GPMG opened fire. The initial burst dropped three of them, and Butch picked off another three before the others disappeared into thick cover.

Yet another blow to Frelimo, but by now the helicopter was getting low on fuel.

Harves let us know he'd be back in an hour or so as he headed back to Gurue.

We returned to the camp.

'You can come out now. Frelimo are gone. You are safe,' Nelson shouted out to Mlando.

People emerged slowly and hesitantly from the shelters. They were nervous seeing soldiers with rifles.

'Mlando! Surezi!' shouted Nelson, 'Tell your people they are safe and that we are friends. Frelimo have been defeated. They are no more!'

The two headmen responded.

I asked Nelson to tell them we would be checking the Frelimo camp to collect weapons, and I didn't mind if they too went into the camp to look for food or other possessions that may be useful to them. They had after all lost everything when abducted from their villages.

Surezi carried an axe he used to access beehives in trees. We asked him to help us enlarge a small clearing at one end of the camp so it would be big enough for the helicopter.

Rex took out a patrol to check on what damage the helicopter had done while we were busy in the initial assault on the camp. He found five bodies.

Twenty-seven killed in the camp attack, plus the five Rex discovered, and plus another three killed in the final helicopter attack. We didn't know exactly how many Frelimo were in the camp, but thirty-five out of forty or fifty was an OK tally and I wasn't unhappy.

We'd started the action at the camp near Gurue ten days earlier. Frelimo didn't know they were being followed and we kept after them for over one hundred kilometres. We took them by surprise again, twice, and inflicted heavy casualties.

The Frelimo cell in northern Nampula had been well and truly destroyed. Dozens of abducted civilians were freed from their slave camps and resettled in protected villages.

Colonel Costa da Silva could relax and make a favourable report to Lisbon.

But we knew it wouldn't last.

The Colonel didn't have the troops to make it last.

Frelimo would be back.

Then so would we.

The Anguish of an SAS General

By March 1980 the situation for the SAS in Rhodesia was untenable. It was clear Mugabe would take power and we didn't want to be around when that happened.

He and the other terrorist leaders had no idea there was an SAS regiment operating against them and we wanted to keep it that way.

Supreme Commander General Peter Walls came to see us at our barracks.

He thanked us for our unwavering professionalism and said he was sorry it all had to end like this.

He said we had three options:

Colonel John Woodhouse, 22 SAS commander at the time, said we would be welcomed by them but would have to complete their Selection Course. The latter was understandable, as we made those coming to us from 22 SAS do the same thing.

To the best of my knowledge nobody in C Squadron took up that offer.

We'd been on operations almost continuously since 1968. The last thing we needed was another selection course and then the prospect of serving in Northern Ireland where we had no expertise.

'Thanks, but No Thanks.' However, it was good of John Woodhouse to make the offer and we appreciated that.

The second offer was to join the newly formed South African special forces known as 'The Recce Commando'.

This was a far better option.

We had got to know the Recce Commando as they had joined us on operations towards the end, particularly with Renamo in Mozambique.

The South Africans offered to take the SAS 'lock, stock and barrel'.

Around two thirds of the unit opted to go to South Africa.

We helped them empty the armouries and load up the Unimogs and Mercedes trucks with all our equipment. The convoy, with wives and family following on in their cars, headed south to the border at Beit Bridge where they were met by the South Africans and escorted to their new home in Durban, Natal.

The rest of us, me included, went for the third option which was to grab what pension money we could, then head off into the big wide world and look for a brand-new start.

I had an offer to join the Sultan's Forces in Muscat and Oman. It was tempting, but I was 33 years old and I'd had more than my fair share of operations. It was time to try something different.

Meanwhile back in Rhodesia General Walls was finding it increasingly lonely at the top.

After the Lancaster House talks Prime Minister Ian Smith walked away from it all, unfairly blaming the General for what he had started with the arrogance of UDI in November 1965.

CIO chief Ken Flower was preparing himself to serve a new master when his wife Olga was suddenly diagnosed with an incurable cancer. The remaining time with her was too precious to waste on the hurly-burly of a country in transition.

General Peter Walls was left on his own.

Left carrying the can.

Trying desperately to make the best out of a seriously bad job.

In the days leading up to the election Mugabe and his ZANU organisation ramped up their presence and efforts in the townships and tribal lands.

There were political rallies, and there was no doubting the level of the support they received from many of the locals.

But not everybody was in favour of Mugabe, and this brought out the true colours of the terrorist group. Public beatings and executions became daily events across the country. Mugabe was intent on winning a landslide victory and he didn't care how he made that happen.

In his office in Salisbury General Peter Walls received the reports of intimidation and brutality. He made sure they reached the British delegation and the Commonwealth troops sent out as observers and peacekeepers. Yet they did nothing.

After the Lancaster House talks the General optimistically believed a free and fair election could take place and that a coalition government would follow.

But as the country closed in on the election date, he finally realised what Smith and most others had figured out months earlier.

Mugabe was going to win a landslide victory.

His country – Rhodesia – would be renamed Zimbabwe – and power would be in the hands of a Chinese-backed terrorist group.

In desperation he made one last appeal to the British.

Surely the British, bastions of western civilisation, wouldn't let this happen?

He wrote a letter to Margaret Thatcher – Prime Minister of Britain.

The letter could not have been more sincere, but the accumulated pressure of the situation certainly clouded his judgement and expectations.

On any other normal day General Peter Walls would have remembered that politicians and diplomats cannot be trusted. None more so than the British, who, with centuries of experience, had developed duplicity into an art form.

In late November 2018 I received a brown envelope with English stamps.

A yellow Post-it note was stuck to the front of several documents.

'Really enjoyed *Secret SAS Missions in Africa*,' it read.

'Enclosed is some material that may be of interest in your future writing.

'Regards. Kevin.'

I knew a couple of Kevins in England and checked with them but this came from somebody else, and I'm eternally grateful.

It was a copy of General Peter Walls' letter to Margaret Thatcher, and the response from England.

I showed the letter to a number of friends and former SAS colleagues. Most responded with words like 'how bloody naïve', and while that's true I think it's a bit churlish.

This was a letter written by a desperate man. A man who had carried massive stress for a long time.

The letter was never going to achieve anything.

It was Peter Walls' last desperate attempt to save a once wonderful country.

And we can't be critical of that.

Letter from General Walls to Margaret Thatcher

cc Mr. Powell FCO
PM has seen
2.3.80

Reply sent.

L. Rnts 3/3

Salisbury
1 March 1980

The Right Honourable Margaret Thatcher, MP
Prime Minister
10 Downing Street
LONDON SW1

Dear Prime Minister

I am exercising the right conferred upon me by you
personally that I have direct access to you when the
situation warrants it. I believe it is my solemn duty
and responsibility to now report to you directly and
make an appeal on behalf of all freedom-loving and
law-abiding Zimbabwe Rhodesians. Many of these have
trusted you and your Government because of my colleagues
and my own example, assurance and encouragement, and in
the case of the security forces, our command. We have
now completed three days of voting as part of the
electoral process agreed at Lancaster House and await
announcement of the results on next Tuesday morning.
I therefore judge this to be the right moment for me
to take this action. I must first explain the background.
Despite your assurance to me that Lord Soames would
measure up to the grave responsibility delegated to him,
I must confirm reports sent to you, through intermediaries,
that he has proved to be inadequate, lacking in moral
courage, lacking in ability to listen and learn, and
above all incapable of implementing the solemn promise,
given by yourself and Lord Carrington, that he would
rely on us for advice on military and other situations,
and act in accordance with the interests of survival
of a moderate, freedom-loving and anti-marxist society.
I will not accuse him of being unwilling to do so,
although many in their bitterness think this to be the
case. He has often treated us as if we had no special
status in your eyes and certainly not as people who,
at great political sacrifice, had agreed to go to the
conference table after militarily forcing the other
parties to agree to do so. It is true his task has not

-2-/...

- 2 -

been made easier by your Government insisting on
unrestricted entry of hundreds of observers and
journalists, many of whom are avowedly left wing
orientated and definitely anti-Muzorewa. Many of
them, and some junior monitors, have been arrogant
enough to set themselves up as instant experts on
this country, and Africa generally, and have made
pronouncements accordingly, contributing greatly to
the emotional and hysterical wave of hostile propaganda
levelled against us. Had the Governor acted resolutely
and effectively in the early days of the pre-election
period, his task would have been much easier, and our
survival as a democratic nation would not now be so
seriously imperilled.

Although it is possible the moderate parties may
achieve acceptable results in the election, I must say
to you in all sincerity and gravity that it will be a
miracle if it happens and in spite of intimidation,
breaches of the ceasefire, and sheer terror accepted
pathetically by your representatives. Although I have
sufficient faith in God to hope that the true wishes
of the people in this country will be manifested some
day in some way and may be even now, I must take the
precaution of making contingency plans for the worst
case on this occasion, especially as reports from all
around the country indicate that massive intimidation
makes a victory by Mugabe the most likely if not
inevitable result of the election.

I should add that many of the affidavits about
intimidation, in the hundreds being forwarded to us
today, have been sworn by your British policemen and
other visitors. I wish you could see the sullen hurt
and misery in the eyes and faces of our black people,
who are normally so cheerful, good-natured, and full
of goodwill.

My appeal to you must be on the following basis :

    (a)   If Mugabe succeeds in gaining a simple
           majority by winning 51 seats or more, or
           if he is able to attract sufficient
           defectors from other parties, it is vital
           to our survival as a free nation that you
           declare the election nul and void on the
           grounds of official reports of massive
           intimidation frustrating the free choice
           of the bulk of the people

-3-/...

- 3 -

   (b) If Mugabe gets less than 50 seats but has
        more than any other party, our present
        efforts to form a coalition based on the
        tripod of Muzorewa, Nkomo and Smith must
        be given every opportunity and help,
        however overt or devious as may be
        necessary, to succeed in governing the
        country and resisting the efforts to
        overthrow them of Mugabe, and anybody
        who supports him

   (c) In the event of the election being
        declared nul and void, or the moderate
        parties failing to form a viable coalition
        with a working majority in the House of
        Assembly, it is essential from my considered
        point of view that you maintain a British
        presence in ZR to run the country with a
        Council of Ministers, thus allowing us to
        provide, if necessary, the military conditions
        for an orderly and safe withdrawal of those
        people of all races who wish to take refuge
        in South Africa or elsewhere. This will be
        preferable to my taking unconstitutional
        action which would be fraught with snags
        and dangers, apart from being loathsome to
        me as a professional soldier, and almost
        certain to result in much bloodshed and
        damage to property, and embarrassment to
        your Government. However, if you are unable
        to see your way to honouring the bond between
        us I must reserve the right to take whatever
        action is necessary in the interests of the
        majority of people whom I am pledged to serve.

It must be without precedent or at least abnormal, for a
person like myself to address such a message as this to no
less than the Prime Minister of Britain, but I wish to
assure you I do so only in the extremity of our possible
emergency, with goodwill, and in the sincere and honest
belief that it is my duty in terms of the privileged
conversations I had with you and Lord Carrington. I don't
know how to sign myself, but I hope to remain your
obedient servant,

PETER WALLS

The British Reply to General Wall's Letter

Unsurprisingly Margaret Thatcher chose not to reply personally to the General's letter.

It was no secret she regarded Rhodesia as 'a tiresome problem', and to be fair to the Iron Lady she had much bigger issues on her plate at the time.

For a start the British economy was in tatters.

The workforce was hostile and disinterested at best.

The rescuing revenue from North Sea oil was yet to arrive.

And on top of these serious domestic problems was the small matter of Argentina's growing interest in reclaiming the Falkland Islands.

The British would wage a very high-risk war for the sake of a dozen or so sheep farmers on these remote Antarctic islands that all logic says should belong to Argentina or Chile.

Yet they wouldn't lift a finger to help Rhodesia.

The British knew all along that Mugabe would seize power and they didn't care.

All that mattered was that Margaret Thatcher would finally be rid of her tiresome problem.

SECRET   2

Foreign and Commonwealth Office

London SW1A 2AH

3 March 1980

Dear Michael,

Rhodesia: Message from General Walls

The Foreign and Commonwealth Secretary discussed with the
Prime Minister yesterday evening the message from General Walls.
Lord Carrington recommends that instructions should be sent as
soon as possible today for the Governor or Sir A Duff to reply
to Walls on the Prime Minister's behalf. The purpose will be to
calm and reassure Walls, without giving hostages to fortune
about the precise composition of the government, or our own role
after the election results are known.

The implied threats in Walls' letter are worrying and no
doubt reflect the strong pressure which Walls is under from
within the armed forces. But he has played a helpful role over
the past week or so both in bringing together the forces of the
two sides and in establishing the foundation for a coalition
between Mr Nkomo, Bishop Muzorewa and the Whites. He will be
aware of the grave consequences of any action to overturn the
election results; and it is unlikely that he has any firm
assurances of South African support. While the risk of hasty
action in the event of a Mugabe landslide undoubtedly exists and
there is evidence of contingency plans in the Rhodesian forces
to deal with the PF in the assembly places, we have no grounds
to think that any action is imminent.

Lord Carrington considers that the Prime Minister's reply
should so far as possible seek to reassure Walls and to recognise
the vital part he has played in recent days. Clearly he cannot
be given any specific commitment about the formation of a
government. But provided Mugabe gets less than 40 seats (ie
short of a majority of the African seats), the sort of coalition
between Nkomo, Muzorewa and the Whites which Walls is seeking
to promote would be a perfectly legitimate objective, though it
might be possible to take some elements of ZANU(PF) into it.
Walls should therefore be reassured that we share the goal of a
broad, moderate and stable government which contributes to
national unity and reconciliation.

/If Mugabe

M O'D B Alexander Esq
10 Downing Street

SECRET

If Mugabe gets more than 40 seats, the situation will be
much more difficult; and it will be hard to avoid a situation
in which he does not have a leading role in the government.
Walls and the Whites could probably be brought to accept some
form of national government, though their suspicion of Mugabe
is such that we should have to approach it carefully, emphasising
the need for unity and reconciliation after the elections and
for a broadly based government which reflected all viewpoints
in the country.

    If Mugabe wins an absolute majority, then our aim will
again have to be a national government in which all parties are
represented, and Mugabe's influence thus diluted. It will be
very difficult to bring the Whites to accept such a government
in which Mugabe would inevitably have a very prominent role,
and the risks of a White reaction would be strongest in these
circumstances. But it is probably the best outcome we could
hope for. Our role in such a case would be difficult. But to
reassure the Whites we would have to indicate that we stood
ready to help with the problems involved in the transition to
independence (though we would not envisage extending the Governor's
stay by more than a matter of days and certainly not beyond
independence).

    I enclose a draft telegram of instructions for the Prime
Minister's approval.

Yours ever

Roderic Lyne

(R M J Lyne)
<u>Private Secretary</u>

OUT TELEGRAM

		Classification and Caveats	Precedence/Deskby
		SECRET	FLASH

ZCZC	1	ZCZC
GRS	2	GRS
CLASS	3	SECRET
CAVEATS	4	
DESKBY	5	
FM FCO	6	FM FCO 031400Z
PRE/ADD	7	TO FLASH SALISBURY
TEL NO	8	TELEGRAM NUMBER
	9	
	10	MY TELNO : RHODESIA: MESSAGE FROM GENERAL WALLS
	11	1. The Prime Minister does not intend to reply to Walls'
	12	message in writing, but would be grateful if you or Sir A Duff
	13	could speak to Walls on the following lines, making clear that
	14	you are doing so on her personal instructions. (In the light
	15	of some of the comments in Walls' message, you may prefer to
	16	ask Sir A Duff to do so).
	17	2. The Prime Minister was glad that Walls felt able to get in
	18	touch with her personally to explain his concerns. She fully
	19	understands what a difficult time this is and in particular
	20	the uncertainty and tension which inevitably exists between
	21	the elections and the declaration of results. She has greatly
///	22	admired the lead taken by Walls in bringing together the forces
//	23	of the two sides and in encouraging co-operation between Nkomo,
/	24	Muzorewa and the Whites, and these efforts have her full support.
	25	

NNNN ends telegram	BLANK	Catchword /The prospects

File number	Dept Rhodesia Dept	Distribution Files PS PS/LPS PS/Mr Luce PS/PUS Mr Day Head, Rhodesia Dept
Drafted by (Block capitals) C D POWELL		
Telephone number 3466		
Authorised for despatch		
Comcen reference	Time of despatch	

XY 48

OUT TELEGRAM (CONT)

		Classification and Caveats SECRET		Page 2

<<<<

1   <<<<

2   The prospects for a peaceful and stable outcome will depend

3   upon others being willing to show the same spirit of

4   reconciliation. The Prime Minister is very grateful to Walls

5   for his outstanding contribution, and hopes that he will

6   continue to do his best to keep all the parties calm during

7   the difficult period ahead.

8   3. It should be made clear to Walls that the Prime Minister

9   regards his criticisms of you as entirely unjustified. The

10 RSF have been deployed fully throughout the interim period and

11 in a way which has enabled them to maintain full control over

12 the military situation. No attempt has been made to interfere

13 with the NJOC's military judgment. The admission of observers

14 to the elections was agreed at Lancaster House. It is also

15 vital to securing international acceptance for Rhodesia.

16 4. You should leave Walls in no doubt that, in the light of

17 the reports from our own supervisors and observers (as well as

18 international groups, the Prime Minister does not share his

19 view that massive intimidation has frustrated the free choice

20 of the people (although she realises that there has been some

21 intimidation) there are no grounds, in the Prime Minister's

22 view, on which the election could be declared null and void.

23 The task now is to make the best of the outcome to ensure a

24 stable government.

25 5. The composition of the future government must, in the

26 Prime Minister's view, reflect the need for unity and

27 reconciliation. It remains her objective, as explained to

28 Walls during the Lancaster House conference, to see Rhodesia brought to

29 independence with as stable and moderate a government as possible

30 which fairly reflects the wishes of the people. The Prime

31 Minister has heard with interest and approval of the

32 discussions which have been taking place between Bishop

33 Muzorewa, Mr Nkomo and the Rhodesian Front, with the

34

NNNN ends telegram	BLANK	Catchword /encouragement

XY 48 A

OUT TELEGRAM (CONT)

| | | Classification and Caveats
SECRET | | Page
3 |

<<<<   1   <<<<

2   encouragement of the NJOC, and hoeps that these can establish
3   the foundations for successful collaboration in the post-
4   election period. Depending on the election results, it may
5   also be necessary to accommodate other parties who are equally
6   prepared to commit themselves to the goals of unity and
7   reconciliation. The Prime Minister has asked the Governor to
8   keep her closely informed of his discussions with the political
9   leaders following the announcement of the election results
10 and will be in touch further with Walls to consider how our
11 common objective of a stable future for Rhodesia can best be
12 achieved. We intend to assist in any way we can with the
13 problems involved in the transition to independence. In the
14 meantime the Prime Minister urges Walls, in the strongest
15 terms, to counsel his colleagues to show calm and restraint;
16 it is only on that basis that we can work successfully together
17 for a government with broad support under which all the people
18 of Rhodesia will continue to feel secure in their future.
19
20 CARRINGTON
21 NNNN

P.M.? (margin annotation near line 10)

| NNNN ends
telegram | BLANK | Catchword |

XY 48 A

A Tribute to General Peter Walls

The first commander of C Squadron SAS died of a heart attack in the airport car park in George, South Africa, on 20 July 2010.

General Peter Walls was a very special man.

Our most recent meeting was when he and his wife Eunice came over to New Zealand in 2005.

I had just bought a new Nissan Patrol and Peter joked that it would have been a great staff car for him. The green I had chosen was even the right colour.

I took Peter and Eunice out to see the gannets at the breeding colony at Muriwai on the wild west coast of Auckland. Everyone in the Rhodesian Army knew I was a birdman so that came as no surprise to them and they loved it.

From the gannet colony we moved inland and had lunch at one of the west Auckland vineyards. Over lunch we discussed the events that led to the end of Rhodesia, and I told Peter how not long after leaving the SAS I had met terrorist leaders Josiah Tongogara and Rex Nyongo at a private party in London.

It started with a silly article alleging atrocities by the Rhodesian Army against civilians that was published by the *Sunday Guardian* – a reputable newspaper but as left in the political spectrum as the *Telegraph* is right.

I did a bit of basic research and established the story originated from a private soldier who had done some undistinguished time in the British army before joining the Rhodesian army.

He took a few innocuous pictures of Lynx aircraft and an RLI Fireforce in action then fabricated a story around them with the clear intent of making a few bucks out of the British media.

He then deserted from the Rhodesian army and headed back to England to promote his nonsense and it was picked up by the *Guardian*.

In response I wrote an angry letter to the editor questioning their motives for publishing such obvious rubbish from a source of equally dubious quality.

I signed the letter as Major M.F Graham: C Squadron Rhodesian SAS: Retired; and was quite happy to include my home contact details.

A few days later I was called by David Martin – the man who had written the article. He chuckled over the phone and said I had written a great letter that would be printed, and he'd love to catch up and maybe buy me a beer if I was ever down in London?

The offer of buying a beer has always worked well with me – as many will testify – and I duly turned up at a Chelsea flat sometime later where an already advanced party was in progress.

David Martin was a larger than life Canadian who was writing a book later published as *The Struggle for Zimbabwe*. I was never cut out to be in the diplomatic corps so I told him in my usual manner that if he wanted any chance of success with his book, he needed to move up a level or two from the pathetic contrived stories of army deserters.

He laughed at that with appreciation and thrust a beer can in my hand. He said he knew all along the story was contrived but it made the paper; at a time in England when left wing liberalism was as dumb as flowers-in-your-hair San Francisco, that apparently was what people wanted to read.

David also said he'd done it for 'friends' who were helping him with his book. He said two of them were at the party and was sure I'd enjoy meeting them.

My surprise showed with a short intake of breath as I learned the first of these was Josiah Tongogara, the ZANU terrorist commander of operations.

He was totally relaxed and laughingly guessed I knew all about him.

'Except for where you were, Josiah!' I responded with a smile as I shook his hand.

'And thank goodness for that,' he replied.

We both laughed, enjoying the unique moment of two adversaries meeting for the first time as people and without threats or weapons.

Josiah Tongogara was one of those charismatic personalities you meet now and then and our short meeting left me with a very positive impression.

Moving across the room I was sat down with Rex Nyongo – later to become Zimbabwe Army Commander. But at that time Rex to me was simply the leader of a terrorist group who had abducted 126 school kids from St Alberts Mission north of Centenary and led them off towards the Zambezi Valley for training at one of their camps.

The bad news for Rex was that the SAS were on hand and we intercepted his group as they began the descent down the steep escarpment into the Zambezi Valley. We got the kids back, killed one of the gang, and Rex Nyongo was incredibly lucky to escape with his life.

Sergeant Andy Chait was one of our stars and a deadly shot. As he squeezed the trigger in the chase Rex fell over a boulder and the shot missed him. He escaped into the night.

At the local Command Centre, I pulled the boys back because I knew where Rex and the survivors of the group would go. We had been looking at this area from the air and had found a camp under cover in an ox-bow on the Musengezi River about fifteen kilometres away. As the last light of that day disappeared, we dropped an ambush group into the camp to await their arrival.

Nothing happened and we pulled the guys out a few days later.

I was bitterly disappointed because I was sure the terrorists would go to the camp.

So, against this background I could not help myself recounting my version of events to Rex Nyongo, who remembered the events remarkably well on top of the half bottle of Scotch already consumed.

Seizing the opportunity, I then asked why he didn't turn up at the camp on the Musengezi where we would have killed him.

It's not every day one gets to ask questions like that.

His eyes lit up and he leaned forward and put his face next to mine.

Breathing whisky fumes over me he exclaimed in that inimitable Zimbabwe accent: 'Ha! I was too clever for you!'

He then collapsed in a bout of sustained laughter, but after some cajoling from me and another slug of whisky I got him to tell me what actually happened.

He admitted he heard the crack of the shot just above his head when he fell over the boulder but then he ran and caught up with the remnants of his terrorist gang. They headed towards the camp on the Musengezi, exactly as we expected.

He asked me if I remembered what the weather was like at the time and I did. It absolutely hosed down; we couldn't fly helicopters and the whole Zambezi Valley was flooded.

While our men waited in ambush just a few metres away Rex was stranded on the opposite side of the river because it was too swollen for them to cross. He said they were very disappointed not to be able to reach the shelter of the camp because they were very cold and wet. They were forced to continue fleeing north to the Zambezi River and did eventually reach a ZANU camp inside Zambia.

He was too drunk to ask anything about me, so I remained anonymous, but Rex Nyongo survived and went on to become Army Commander of Zimbabwe.

Peter Walls loved this story and in response to my positive regard for Tongogara said that he too had similar respect for the man.

They apparently got to know each other well enough for Tongogara to exclaim, at one of the many peace meetings with the British, that while the political aspirants were squabbling amongst themselves, they should leave things to him and Peter. The two of them would soon bring peace and stability to Rhodesia.

Peter thought that was a sincere ambition rather than one that was politically motivated, so I relate this because I think our SAS General got closer than anyone to achieving a coalition that would probably have worked and saved many lives in Rhodesia.

It was not to be of course, because Tongogara was assassinated in his car and the main threat to Mugabe taking power was thus removed.

We also discussed the events at the very end of Rhodesia.

As the 1980 election results unfolded, the SAS and others were poised to intervene in what would essentially have been a military coup. It would have been a very bloody coup and for many obvious reasons was unlikely to have succeeded for any length of time.

The General did the right thing and said no to the proposed coup.

It was the right decision but he took a lot of flak from combat unit commanders and their men, and many in the SAS also felt aggrieved.

As the first commander of C Squadron he said this reaction from the SAS was upsetting to him.

I told him what I have told everyone else who raises the subject:

Those who supported the coup operation were too caught up in the emotion and stress of a long battle to be realistic. Refusing to allow it to happen was the only sensible decision to make, and Peter had the courage to make it in what were extremely difficult and emotional times.

I was disappointed with Ian Smith's version of events in his boring biography and I will never accept his criticism of Peter Walls. Smith threw in the towel because he had lost control long before the end. Our SAS General was left with the unenviable job of closing an unfortunate chapter in history that Smith started with UDI on 11 November 1965. He did it well and with dignity.

South Africa's Zimbabwe Flop

In his book *Serving Secretly*, CIO chief Ken Flower would have us believe he was sincere in telling Mugabe that the South Africans would never be stupid enough to try destabilising Zimbabwe.

Well sorry Ken, you can't seriously expect us to swallow that.

It was after all Ken Flower who set up the propaganda radio, who organised the SAS to train Renamo in Mozambique, and who was fully informed of their success against communist Frelimo.

And as the end drew nigh in Zimbabwe it was the same Ken Flower who orchestrated the management transfer of Renamo to the South African intelligence service and on the ground replaced the SAS with the South African Special Forces, the 'Recce Commando'.

Finally, Ken Flower knew full well that a big contingent of SAS had gone south to join the Recce Commando.

Ken Flower would not have been privy to South African intentions, but a man of his experience and ability must have realised they would give the Renamo concept a try in Zimbabwe. Especially when at least a third of the country, in the form of the Ndebele tribe and their Russian sponsored ZAPU terrorist group, were strongly opposed to Mugabe.

Personally, I think it was one of those 'hot potatoes' he prudently chose to withhold from Mugabe.

The South African action against Zimbabwe started in December 1980, and to tell us all about it was Karate.

Karate was the one member of my SAS team Sierra One Seven who had opted to join the Recce Commando. He'd served with them for another six years, leaving in December 1986 and now he'd come to New Zealand to see me and his old mate Pig Dog.

My crooked-tooth right-hand man hadn't changed much as I met him off the Qantas flight from Sydney. I led him to the domestic terminal where an Air New Zealand flight would take us south to the town of New Plymouth and the big volcano Mount Taranaki.

I'd booked us into the Mountain Lodge located high on the slopes of the mountain. It was run by a Swiss family and only had six rooms. I had booked three of them.

I saw a battered looking green Toyota Hilux in the car park and correctly guessed Pig Dog had got there before us.

That afternoon I suggested we take a walk on one of the bush tracks leading up the mountain. It was great weather and the snow-capped volcano was looking spectacular, but I'd seen the mountain forecast and it was about to change.

The track climbed through Mountain Beech forest which turned into shrubs and tussock grass as we ascended. Out in the open we could see forever.

To the east of us on the horizon were the snow-capped peaks of the three really big volcanoes; Ruapehu, Tongariro and Ngauruhoe. Karate had never seen anything like it in his life.

After dinner we changed into togs and met in the spa room. Karate had bought a big bottle of Drambuie at Duty Free and brought that along with three glasses.

We settled into the warm water then one of the staff came in to dim the interior lighting and turn on the outside floodlights. A floor-to-ceiling glass wall revealed beech trees, tree ferns and alpine shrubs. It was stunning. And then to cap it all it started to snow.

For a while we just sat in the hot water and marvelled at the spectacle.

Pig Dog got out of the spa, topped up the glasses with Drambuie, then said:

'OK Karate. Tell us what happened. Right from the start when you all left Rhodesia in the convoy.'

Karate gathered his thoughts.

'At the start,' he said, 'it was all very new and exciting, especially for the families. The barracks at the Recce Commando were amazing. We each had a bedroom and small living room with a TV. The married members had small houses with a garden and garage. There was a local school and the sports facilities were second to none.

'But this initial excitement didn't last long. As we were integrated into their companies a serious problem emerged.

'A few of their officers and several of their senior NCOs would only speak Afrikaans. So those of us who couldn't speak the language went through briefings and training exercises without having a clue what was being said.

'We weren't slow to voice our concern and I thought the boys did it well. They explained they were committed to learning Afrikaans, but you can't learn a new language overnight, and meanwhile could they accommodate us with a bit of English?

'It couldn't have been more reasonable and we sensed that ninety per cent of the Recce boys were with us, but a hard-nosed warrant officer who we reckon was still fighting the Boer War replied with something that was abusive in Afrikaans.

'Big Sergeant Joe Van Vuuren, who spoke Afrikaans, responded in kind and warned the guy if he heard anything like that again he'd wake up in hospital.

'Joe was bristling and would have smashed the South African, who then made the mistake of trying to pull rank.

'Fuck you,' said Joe and moved in for the kill.

'Everyone then intervened to stop the altercation and we went our own ways.

'Later a delegation of the SAS team went to see the Colonel who had heard about the ruckus.

'He was sympathetic and suggested the best thing would be to get us deployed back into the field as soon as possible.

'Eighteen of us, me included, were dropped back into Mozambique with Renamo, while the remainder were moved up to the Rhodesian border, next to the Limpopo River.

'I was amazed at how well things were going for Renamo. They had moved a long way from where we started in Gorongoza and Sitatonga. To the north Afonso Dhlakama had established himself in the Malawi foothills, not far from where we bombed that big Frelimo camp in the Furuncungo operation.

'We heard South Africa was keeping Malawi president Dr Hastings Banda on side with a generous aid package. They needed his help with Renamo and also with labour for their mines.

'I was dropped by helicopter well south of the Buzi River where we captured the electricity company's Land Cruiser. I was met by Phillip and was pleased to see the vehicle still going strong. Your paint job was just as bad, Mick,' he added.

We all laughed. The Land Cruiser was white when we captured it so I ordered pots of green and brown paint that we daubed all over the vehicle. It was rough, but better than white.

'The South Africans wanted us to focus on recruitment and spread south towards Maputo as fast as we could. We had the occasional skirmish with Frelimo but nothing major as it was all about recruitment and training before the big battles to come.

'After nine weeks in the field I had some R and R and caught up with a few of the boys back at base.

'The South Africans set up a semi-permanent base camp in a game reserve and game ranching area known as the Tuli Block. It is close to where the borders of South Africa, Botswana and Zimbabwe meet. Over one hundred men were based there, mainly SAS but also a number of African soldiers, many from the Rhodesian Selous Scouts.

'From this base they conducted regular recce patrols across the border, and it soon became obvious the South Africans were well organised in Zimbabwe, with trucks and cars hidden in the bush.

'The first raid took place in December 1980 and involved six of our SAS men.

'They were dressed in civilian clothes and used one of the cars to drive up to Harare where they booked into a motel. They said how casual it was wandering the streets of Harare and visiting the old haunts.

'On the second afternoon they met a senior NCO from the RLI – Rhodesian Light Infantry – a white guy. He said he would meet them on the roadside just short of the entrance to the barracks at around 2030 hours that night.

'The NCO went to the RLI truck yard, signed for a five-tonne Mercedes truck, and made sure it was fully fuelled.

'As you will remember the RLI had three commando units plus a support group with mortars and each had their own armoury.

'At 1830 hours he drove the truck to 1 Commando where he told the armourer – a corporal – that he'd been ordered by Army HQ to collect up all the weapons urgently "so the bloody kaffirs can't get their hands on them".

'The armourer swallowed the story from his superior and helped load the weapons into the truck. He then repeated the exercise at the other three locations and in a couple of hours he'd cleaned out the weapon stock of the RLI – about a quarter million bucks worth!

'They met as planned and one of the lads jumped into the truck with him. They drove through the night into Matabeleland and then on the bush roads back to the camp on the Limpopo.

'They unloaded all the weapons and even managed to winch the Merc truck across the river, so they got that as well.

'The RLI NCO involved joined the Recces and was still there when I left. We reckon he was well paid for his exploits as it wasn't long before he turned up with a brand-new VW Jetta.'

Pig Dog put his head back and laughed out loud.

'What a ripper!' he cried.

'My God, I would have given anything to be a fly on the wall when the brass found out next day. Poor bloody corporals though. I bet it wasn't funny for them.'

We sat up on the edge of the spa to cool down as the snow continued falling outside.

Karate resumed the story.

'The second operation was launched a few weeks later. This time a team took explosives with them and again drove up to Harare.

'They got into King George VI Barracks and laid charges on thirty trucks. Whoever did it screwed up with the initiation set because the charges didn't blow, but you can imagine the panic when they found all the explosives the following morning.

'Their next target was the huge arsenal at Inkomo Barracks outside Harare where tons of weapons, mines and other explosives had been accumulated after the cease fire. Intelligence suggested all these weapons and mines were to be donated to the ANC.

'This would be a serious threat to South Africa and had to be neutralised.

'The task of removing the threat was given to Captain Patrick Gericke.

'Gericke was a military engineer and a trained covert operator so this time there were no cock-ups.

'He was faced with a difficult task because Inkomo was a massive site with the magazine bunkers all well spread out – much too big to contemplate blowing everything with conventional demolition techniques.

'Patrick Gericke's ingenuity was amazing. The collected arms and munitions such as TM-46 landmines were at first housed at a temporary location before being moved to the safety of the magazines at Inkomo. Gericke skilfully managed to access the temporary site where he then inserted specially made 6-month delay timers into many of the landmines.

'The Zimbabwe military then obliged by taking everything to the magazines, unwittingly spreading the infected mines across the site. Each of the ticking time bombs contained nearly 6kg of TNT – more than enough to get everything else going when it detonated.

'And it all worked to perfection, resulting in the destruction of arms, ammunition, shells and explosives worth in excess of $50million, and in the process denying the ANC the opportunity of escalating their activities inside South Africa.'

'That is incredible,' I said. I knew the site, and as one of the SAS explosives experts immediately recognised the difficulty in trying to destroy such an extensive complex. What Patrick Gericke achieved was pure genius.

'But he ran into a snag down the line,' Karate continued.

'He'd somehow attracted the attention of the CIO and was later arrested and taken to jail.

'He would almost certainly have been executed were it not for the fact that the local Police Inspector – one Fred Varkevisser – was also on the South African payroll. He released Gericke and the two of them, with support from a team from South Africa who were specifically tasked with the rescue operation, fled the country in a light aircraft.'

'Amazing,' said Pig Dog. 'I thought we got up to some pretty tricky things, but these stories make our action look like a walk in the park.'

'But all these operations only involved a few men. What about the others? What were the rest up to at that camp on the Limpopo?' I asked.

Karate continued.

'They said that deeper patrols into Matabeleland commenced and some made contact with ZAPU groups, many of whom had avoided the camps set up after the war, and had kept their weapons.

'But Mick, what struck me was the South Africans made no effort to copy what was being done with Renamo in Mozambique. There was no radio station pushing out propaganda, no hearts and minds or any other campaign to rally the Ndebele and ZAPU against Mugabe.

'Instead they seemed to be putting all their effort into supporting small dissident ZAPU groups, and that was never going to work. For a start there were big divisions within ZAPU. One of their chiefs – Emmerson Mnangagwa – defected to join Mugabe, and Mugabe had spies everywhere.

'As our Renamo force in Mozambique grew into thousands strong I could never see anything like it ever happening in Zimbabwe. And it didn't. Just the opposite in fact.'

And on that sobering note we called it quits for what had been a remarkable day at the Mountain House.

The following day the Mountain House was enveloped in cloud. It was windy and cold and a few snowflakes still drifted down. The staff had lit a big fire in the lounge so we settled into three comfortable armchairs, ready for Karate to resume his story.

'I don't know how much the South Africans had to do with it but the next major event was in early 1981 when a ZAPU faction of about 2,000 guerrillas based outside Bulawayo on the Victoria Falls road rebelled.

'They had a few Russian BTR 152 Armoured Personnel Carriers and started the action by attacking a pro-Mugabe faction being trained by British Army instructors.

'They attacked the camp after the instructors had left in the evening, killing twelve and scattering the rest.

'They then headed towards Bulawayo where they were engaged by the white officer-led Rhodesian African Rifles and elements of the new Zimbabwe National Army. In the action that followed, over 400 ZAPU were killed, many more surrendered and even more disappeared into the bush fearing reprisals.

'Mugabe publicly attacked the ZAPU element, saying they were disloyal, misguided and political malcontents. He said there had been a definite organised pattern to the rebellion.

'I think this is the first clue indicating that he knew something was a foot in Matabeleland.

'The next operation was something of a red herring because it had nothing to do with ZAPU and wasn't in Matabeleland, and this definitely involved our SAS boys.

'In July 1982 a team of six drove to Gwelo in a car. The boot was full of explosives and accessories.

'I wasn't ever told who at the Thornhill airbase helped them, but somebody must have because the air force police there had guard dogs.

'On the night of 25 July, they blew up thirteen newly delivered Hawk jet fighter trainers from Britain, jumped back into their car and once again disappeared into the bush, leaving no clue as to who was responsible.

'Yes,' I said, 'but Mugabe arrested four air force officers, including the base commander Hugh Slatter and my good friend Pete Briscoe – the helicopter pilot. Pete was the pilot when we flew with that tame hyena. Will never forget him taking off calmly as the big hairy animal licked the sweat off the back of his neck.

'Both Pete and Hugh were intelligent men but they wouldn't have a clue about blowing up anything. This operation had SAS written all over it.'

'It did,' agreed Karate.

'Maybe it was a smokescreen to deflect attention away from what they were doing closer to Bulawayo,' offered Pig Dog, and that too was a realistic possibility.

Karate agreed. 'Yes, I think you are right Pig Dog because, coincidentally, a week or two before the aircraft were destroyed, the Recce Commando promoted our SAS hero Darrel Watt to the rank of major and put him in charge of the base on the Limpopo River.

'Darrel of course had intimate knowledge of Renamo operations towards the end of our campaign, and having hunted in this area on many occasions he also knew the bush as well as anyone. It made sense then for the South Africans to put him in charge of getting a Renamo-style uprising going in Matabeleland.

'He was helped in this by a network of South African paid informers, and for a while it looked like the intelligence was OK and they made progress. The ZAPU groups they met were authentic and full of hatred for Mugabe.

'In May 1981 Darrel sent out a patrol of eighteen men to meet a ZAPU group at a river junction some sixty kilometres inland from the border. The plan was to get them to grow a gang hidden in the bush. Darrel would provide the arms and rations until they were ready to strike against Mugabe.

'It took them three days to reach the rendezvous point. Patrol leader SAS man Dave Berry put the group in cover while he and ex-RLI commandos Rob Beech and John Wessells, and former Selous Scout Khiwa, went forward to recce the area and make sure it was safe.

'Mugabe had learned about this proposed meeting and had sent two infantry platoons to set up an elaborate ambush position at the river junction.

'Dave and the recce party unwittingly walked into the ambush position and were gunned down. All four were killed.

'The ambush group then commenced a search for the others who managed to avoid contact and eventually returned safely to the Limpopo base with the bad news.'

'For God's sake!' cried Pig Dog. 'The SAS don't get caught in ambushes and Dave Berry was a good operator.'

'Yes,' said Karate. 'Everybody said that. All they could think of was that Dave had already met the ZAPU gang in question so wasn't expecting any surprises.

'And it got worse. Mugabe's troops took the bodies of the four men and paraded them on the front of vehicles that were driven around Bulawayo and the townships. Eventually we understand they were dumped down a disused mineshaft on the outskirts of town.

'And meanwhile Mugabe sent troops into Bulawayo to raid a number of properties associated with ZAPU. They found concealed arms and explosives. More bodies joined Dave Berry and crew at the bottom of the mineshaft.

'It was a bad time for Darrel and the South Africans.'

We took a break for some coffee and to reflect on what Karate had told us.

I patted Pig Dog on the shoulder. 'Listening to all this I reckon we both made a bloody good call to make a new life somewhere else.'

'Can't argue with that,' he replied with a grin. 'And I would never have got on with those South Africans.'

We settled down again in front of the fire.

'The killing of Dave Berry was widely reported in the international press and I followed it here with much interest,' I started out to get things going again.

'From the reports I read, and from other material that surfaced later, it was clear to me that the South Africans didn't have the monopoly on intelligence they thought they had. They called their operation against Zimbabwe 'Operation Drama' and with a network of paid informers and dissident ZAPU groups were confident they would be successful.

'The problem was that Robert Mugabe had already worked out exactly what was going on.

'He didn't need paid informers. All the answers were readily available by simply looking at Mozambique.

'Before the Portuguese exodus from Mozambique the Chinese encouraged Frelimo leader Samora Machel to allow ZANU terrorist groups to join them at their training camps. Frelimo readily agreed and were strong supporters of ZANU. This relationship allowed them to train in relative safety, and later, when the Portuguese left Africa it gave them access to over 800 kilometres of Rhodesian border.

'The South Africans already knew Zimbabwe had welcomed their ANC, and new leader Mugabe realised they would not want a similar relationship developing with the ANC in his country. Which would explain the raids and attacks on the aircraft that were clearly aimed at disrupting Zimbabwe, and their military in particular.'

Karate and Pig Dog nodded in agreement. 'Mick, it looks like you never stopped being the intelligence man,' laughed Karate. 'But it all makes sense.'

'Mozambique also revealed the answer to the increasing problem of dissent in Matabeleland,' I continued.

'Frelimo leader Samora Machel had been to see Mugabe and told him how Renamo, with ever increasing aid from South Africa, had grown from a bunch of rebels into a well organised opposition. The situation in Mozambique had now deteriorated into all-out civil war.

'Machel asked Mugabe for assistance with troops and fighting vehicles. Mugabe agreed but said it would follow only when he had got his own house in order.

'Knowing that South Africa was sponsoring the conflict in Mozambique, Mugabe didn't need another degree to work out that the South Africans were trying the same trick in Matabeleland with dissident ZAPU terrorist groups, and he swung into action.

'More on that later, but what happened at the Recce Commando after Dave Berry and the others were killed?' I asked, passing the baton back to Karate.

'Well, I understand Darrel didn't have a clue what to do next, because it was obvious to him their efforts were being compromised and that had already cost four lives. He was told to stay and he busied everybody by constructing defensive positions at the base and by doing daily wide-ranging clearance patrols.

'He thought the Zimbabwe trackers would have followed them to the base and that the Zimbabwe army might launch an attack. That was a realistic possibility so it kept everybody busy while events unfolded in Pretoria.

'Isolated as he was up there on the border, Darrel at first had no idea that in response to the international media reports of the killings the SADF blamed him for the incident. Head of the SADF, General Constand Viljoen, claimed the group were on an unauthorised mission to rescue political detainees held in a camp in Matabeleland.

'Colonel Jan Breytenbach, commander of Operation Drama, confirmed the mission had been authorised by Major Darrel Watt, and that he had no authority to send troops across the border without the approval of his superiors. Darrel was called to Pretoria to face disciplinary action, and he left the SADF immediately thereafter for a much more sensible job managing a game reserve in Zambia.'

'Arrrgh! I can't believe what I'm hearing,' cried Pig Dog. 'Bastards!'

'Yes,' said Karate. 'All the Recce boys knew that Darrel was acting on orders. Most ex-Rhodesians resigned and left at that point.

'But it didn't end there,' continued Karate. 'The SADF issued false death certificates that were so amateurish the next of kin immediately questioned them through the media. The certificates said the three white soldiers had died from 'multiple injuries' while in contact with the enemy "in Pretoria" for goodness sake!'

'Arrrgh!' repeated Pig Dog.

'Oh yes and they didn't ever issue a death certificate for Khiwa,' added Karate.

'Just another kaffir. That really bugged me when I heard about it, given we had been living with the Renamo boys for some years by then and had got very close to them.'

'Let's go for a walk,' I said as we were all wound up and pretty emotional.

When we got back, I asked Pig Dog and Karate if they had heard of *Gukurahundi*.

'It means something like *the early rains that wash away the chaff*,' I added. They hadn't.

'Well, it involved Mugabe's Fifth Brigade – which you will have heard of,' I continued.

'After the killing of Dave Berry and the others, were there any other operations that you know of into Matabeleland?' I asked Karate.

'Don't think so,' he replied.

'So, the killings effectively ended the South African Operation Drama. Mugabe would have been pleased with that,' I continued. 'But he'd not yet got to the root of the problem, which was the continued existence of ZAPU gangs in Matabeleland, and their political representation in his government.

'Mugabe had got to know North Korean leader Kim Il Sung and turned to him for assistance. He said he needed a militia 'to control malcontents'. The Korean leader responded by sending 106 military instructors to Zimbabwe.

'The members of the Fifth Brigade were drawn from 3,500 ex-ZANU troops, and their training lasted until September 1982. It was different from all other Zimbabwean army units in that it was directly subordinated to the Prime Minister's office, and not integrated with the normal army command structures.

'Their codes, uniforms, radios and equipment were not compatible with other army units.

'Mugabe had created his own palace guard – his own special forces – especially trained in the art of brutal subjugation of any local population.

'It was a master stroke on his part,' I said.

'He kicked off the offensive by calling ZAPU leader Joshua Nkomo "a cobra in the house" and expelled him from parliament. The other elected ZAPU parliamentarians were arrested and handed over to the Fifth Brigade.

'The Brigade moved into Bulawayo and began a five-year purge against the Ndebele people, starting with local ZAPU officials and veterans of ZAPU's armed wing.

'Seizure or detention by the Fifth Brigade was arbitrary. Men of fighting age were considered potential dissidents and therefore guilty of subversive activities.

'Most detained were summarily executed or marched to re-education camps. Most of the dead were shot in public executions, often after being forced to dig their own graves in front of family and fellow villagers. On occasions the Fifth Brigade also massacred large groups of Ndebele, seemingly at random. The largest such incident occurred in March 1983, when sixty-two young men and women were shot near Lupane.

'The casualty figures from this campaign vary from a conservative 8,000 deaths to in excess of 20,000. Nobody will ever know.

'I said it was a master stroke by Mugabe because *Gukurahundi* achieved what he'd probably been thinking about ever since the first election day in April 1980.

'Firstly, the demise of ZAPU in Matabeleland at the hands of the Fifth Brigade removed once and for all time any possibility of the South Africans sponsoring an uprising.

'Secondly, the Ndebele, whose Chief Lobengula had subjugated and plundered Mugabe's Mashona tribe a hundred years earlier, were reduced, whipped and finally put in their place.

'Thirdly he had eliminated the opposition party – ZAPU – from government. His party – ZANU – would be the single player in the one-party state these moves had created.

'Fourthly, with the Fifth Brigade Mugabe had his own Special Forces. It would keep the ZANU military commanders on their toes and in line.

'And finally, it made him the supreme power in Zimbabwe.

'Mugabe was King!'

And he was about to extract a King's ransom.

Epilogue

At the end of apartheid in South Africa new president Nelson Mandela ordered the formation of a 'Truth and Reconciliation Commission' in an effort to heal old wounds.

The Dave Berry killing was reviewed by the Commission.

It found as follows:

'The Commission finds that the SADF's public description of the mission as unauthorised was misleading and not a full and proper description. It was unfair to those who participated in it and insensitive particularly to the families of those who died in it.

'The Commission recommends therefore, that the SADF issue an official acknowledgement that all those who participated in this operation, did so in the belief that they were acting in terms of properly authorised commands, and that those who died did so in what they believed was their line of duty.

'Such a statement should be made public and placed in the personal files of all the participants. It is also recommended that correct death certificates be issued to the next of kin of the deceased and placed in their personal files.'

Renamo Gather Steam

As interesting as the Zimbabwe situation was, what I really wanted to hear about from Karate was the progress with rebel group Renamo in Mozambique. It was, after all, our team that got them going, with Rex heading north into the Gorongoza area with one group, while I went south to my birdwatching hot spot of Sitatonga with the others.

Karate had been with me and returned to continue operations in the southern area.

He picked up the story.

'Mick, I remember you saying it was inevitable that sooner or later Frelimo would find out our bases were in Gorongoza and Sitatonga. Gorongoza especially because of its relatively close proximity to Chimoio and Inhaminga where Rex and Andre made the first attacks.

'Well that's what happened, but not before Afonso had sent small groups away to recruit on the Malawi border, and also due east into the lower Zambezi province of Sofala, where the Shire River from Malawi joins the Zambezi. He told us how surprised they had been to find another small local anti-Frelimo resistance movement there, whom they quickly made part of Renamo, and shared the arms and supplies that were by now pouring in from South Africa.

'Mick, we taught them well, because Afonso and the others in our original groups never forgot the basic principles of guerrilla warfare we explained to them:

'Better to keep moving.

'Better to stay in small groups and disperse far and wide.

'Stretch the resources of the enemy to breaking point.

'Afonso and his remaining men got word that Frelimo were about to mount a major offensive against Gorongoza mountain with Russian tanks and artillery.

'He got one party to take all the weapons they had recently received and hide them in a cache deep inside the mountain complex, and then immediately head north and set up a new base north of the Inyanga Mountains on the Zimbabwe border.

'He meanwhile took another party south to the Gorongoza settlement that he correctly guessed would be the Frelimo staging point for an attack on the mountain. They laid mines in the road and anti-personnel mines in the surrounding area, then in the Isuzu truck they had captured at Inhaminga drove away in the night.

'They crossed the main Beira–Umtali road and kept going south, hiding in the day and only driving at night, until they eventually reached our camp at Sitatonga.

'Frelimo meanwhile obligingly hit the mines and immediately mounted an elaborate attack with their heavy weapons on the mountain, only to find the birds had flown.

'Afonso returned to Gorongoza Mountain some time later as he regarded it as the spiritual home of Renamo, but after the attack he realised that Frelimo were increasingly reliant on the armour and heavy weapons from Russia, and in so doing were bound to their bases and roads.

'They had lost the ability to fight a guerrilla war.

'He remembered we had told him this as well when describing how the SAS put ZAPU out of the race for Zimbabwe by blowing the bridges in Zambia and halting their advance. He reminded everybody about this at Sitatonga and urged us to attack the roads and railway lines Frelimo were now dependent on.

'It was also good to have him there for another reason.

'The South Africans were pressing us to head south towards the Mozambique capital of Maputo. They wanted us to increase our recruiting campaign along the border, and to help with this had flown in over a hundred illegal immigrants from Mozambique they had rounded up in South Africa. These men weren't given any options. They were put in uniform and given a month's basic training at a camp at Pilgrim's Rest before being flown in by helicopter to join Renamo.

'Afonso could see the logic behind the South African demands, but was wise enough to insist he went about it his way.

'Phillip and some of the other locals from the Buzi River area knew the country along the border to the south and told Afonso it was unsuitable for Renamo operations. The Gaza province, as it was known, was very hot sandy country, mostly open with scattered patches of low sandalwood trees, and there was no water.

'"No water, no cover, no people, no use to Renamo!" said Afonso.

'They suggested that instead of following the border they should head east and into the coastal province of Inhambane. There was a national park known as Zinave that would be a safe base area from which they could send out recruiting parties into the populated coastal zone.

'Afonso agreed at once because he also knew that in this same area were the main roads and railway line linking capital Maputo with the rest of Mozambique to the north. Destroying these would do major damage to Frelimo. It would force them to redeploy troops and weapons to the area, and such troop movements could also be seriously disrupted by mining the roads and blowing bridges.

'The South Africans liked the idea and suggested a joint operation. While Afonso blew the bridges and ambushed the roads in the northern part of Inhambane, they would send in teams from the Recce Commando to destroy the road and rail bridges closer to the capital Maputo.

'In the weeks that followed we made a camp in the Zinave Game Reserve. It was a good place. We could reach it via a rough track that was OK for the truck and the land cruiser, there was plenty of water in the Sabi River on the northern boundary, and no people.

'At first, we did some recce work.

'About 100 kilometres from our base towards the coast, the main road and railway line between Maputo and Beira crossed the Sabi River. The bridges were obvious targets so Afonso and I took a party in the Land Cruiser to have a look and work out what we would need to bring them down.

'The railway bridge consisted of steel arches between concrete piers. I decided I'd use plastic explosive "cutting charges" on the two main steel I-beams, in conjunction with a big charge to lift the structure off the piers and let gravity and momentum do the rest. Just as we did on the Zambian bridges.

'The road bridge was similar to the Zambian bridges but accessibility was simple and there was plenty of room under the concrete slabs to lay the charges.

'Because we knew the Recce Commando would be doing similar damage to the south of us, Afonso decided that any Frelimo reaction would come from the north, so he went about organising a substantial ambush of the road.

'We let the South Africans know what we wanted and a C-130 flew in one afternoon to deliver the goods.

'In addition to the explosives, Afonso had ordered mortar bombs, ammunition for the 14.5mm gun we had captured at Inhaminga, and some shells for the recoilless rifle. He was hoping a good sized contingent of Frelimo would turn up so he could use them all.

'And while all this was going on Afonso also organised an attack on the pipeline close to Beira that fed fuel and oil to Zimbabwe. The Shire River group went south to do this.

'He ordered the group he'd sent north from Gorongoza to attack the small Frelimo garrison at Nyamapanda on the border with Zimbabwe and on the road to Tete.

'And finally, he ordered the group on the border with Malawi to mount a night mortar attack on the town of Tete.'

'Brilliant!' I said. 'Multiple attacks all at roughly the same time from Tete on the Zambezi River in the north, so close to their capital in the south. Nearly a thousand kilometres between attacks. Amazing!'

'How many men did Afonso have at that stage?' I asked.

'Not sure,' answered Karate. 'I don't think Afonso knew either but we guessed at around eight thousand.'

'Still massively outnumbered by Frelimo,' I said, 'but it doesn't matter when you are fighting a guerrilla war like this. After these attacks Frelimo would be thinking Renamo was ten times bigger than it actually was. Keeping them guessing is all part of the game.

'So how did it all pan out?' I asked eagerly.

'Couldn't have gone better,' replied Karate.

'In the north the Renamo group overran the small Frelimo garrison at Nyamapanda. Twelve Frelimo were killed and the rest fled across the border into Zimbabwe. They captured another truck and another 14.5mm gun, and after looting the place they set fire to everything. Before leaving in their new truck they hoisted the Renamo flag on the flag pole.

'The attack on Tete sounded a bit like that attack we did on Mague when the anti-aircraft guns were firing their tracer into the night sky. They mortared Tete intermittently over a period of two hours, and every time they fired it prompted a firework show from Frelimo. They must have used thousands of rounds of ammunition.

'The pipeline to Zimbabwe was blown up and that stopped all fuel going to Mugabe for some time.

'On the Sabi River, Afonso positioned his ambush on the north bank, while I laid charges with Phillip and a couple of others on the two bridges.

'We laid the charges at night and were not disturbed. It was an enjoyable demolition job but my dilemma was when to initiate. I kept thinking how cool it would be to blow the bridge just as a train came along, but eventually decided against it because that could be days away.

'I put a good length of safety fuse on both bridges so we had plenty of time to get well clear of the danger area. With steel from the railway bridge flying around we needed to be well away.

'You would have been proud of me, Mick,' he said. 'Both bridges dropped cleanly off the piers, and I got my wish about the train. The following day one came along and at full steam ahead went straight into the river. There was a massive tangle of derailed freight carriages behind the engine. It would be a nightmare clearing it all up.

'During the day traffic started to build up at the broken bridge. A fuel tanker truck arrived and Afonso gave it a burst from the 14.5mm gun. It exploded into flames as the tracer struck home. I don't think anyone was injured but it had the desired effect of getting rid of the people who had been milling around at the edge of the bridge.

'Ha!' laughed Pig Dog. 'I bet it did!'

'Meanwhile to the south of us I later learned the Recce Commando had been up to similar tricks closer to Maputo.

'They came in off submarines and used medium sized zodiacs to get into the coast.

'On the same night as I blew the bridges over the Sabi they dropped another two rail and two road bridges over rivers further south.

'And at the same time a helicopter team flew in across the Kruger National Park to blow a bridge across the Letaba River on the railway line to Zimbabwe – further isolating Zimbabwe and Mugabe.

'Finally, on the third day, Frelimo eventually arrived at Afonso's ambush.

'Realising the Frelimo would be well spread out, some distance behind tanks or armoured personnel carriers that would lead the way, he split his ambush party. He put mines in the road then concealed the recoilless rifle and several men with RPGs off to one side and some distance back from the mines.

'His main ambushing party with the mortars and 14.5mm gun, he took several hundred metres up the road away from the bridge.

'It was hoped the lead Frelimo vehicle would strike a mine and become immobilised. At that point the recoilless rifle would engage the next vehicle behind it.

'Once the action up front started, Afonso would then engage the rear echelons of Frelimo. And that's exactly what happened.

'They had three T-54 tanks leading the way. The front one hit a mine that blew off a track. The blast probably stunned the crew, and it came to a grinding halt. As that happened the recoilless rifle hit the second tank. The round hit where the turret swivelled and did serious damage. They reloaded and hit the tank again twice, putting it out of action.

'The third tank fired its main gun at no particular target, then reversed away from the action, never to be seen again. The recoilless rifle and the RPGs then fired on the stranded lead tank and destroyed that.

'Afonso meanwhile had positioned his men to perfection. As the lead tank detonated the mine, his group opened fire on the Frelimo column advancing behind the armour. The 14.5mm gun did massive damage, and as the Frelimo troops tried to escape from their trucks, the mortars arrived with deadly effect.

'Renamo kept firing. Once they got started it was nigh impossible to stop them. We thought it was probably a local company of Frelimo sent to investigate the bridge demolitions – around 100 men. At least half perished in the ambush and all their vehicles were destroyed.'

'Unbelievable!' I said. 'That would have been a massive blow to Frelimo. Samora Machel must have been a worried man. He was being defeated and neither he nor his Soviet advisers had a clue what to do about it.'

'Yes, that's true,' replied Karate.

'In desperation he turned to Zimbabwe and Mugabe for help, while at the same time he sent some of his troops to Tanzania to retrain in the art of guerrilla warfare.

'That didn't come to anything but the Zimbabweans entering the conflict in Mozambique had a profound impact.

'Remember this was a time when they still had Rhodesian army officers and men, mainly ex–RAR. They had been through the Rhodesian bush war and were seasoned veterans. They were good – too good for Renamo – but it didn't matter. There were not many of them and they couldn't be everywhere.

'And Afonso never forgot what we told him:

'Stay in small groups,

'Keep moving,

'Stretch the enemy's resources to breaking point.

'I stayed with them in the southern area until 1986, and we continued to have good success against Frelimo. But then I was called back to base in Durban where I was given a special mission. It was to be my last, but that story is going to have to wait until tomorrow. The bar is now open and I feel as if I have been talking all day!'

Pig Dog and I both agreed and thanked him for sharing his stories. I said there would be many questions we'd want to ask but doing that over a beer or two would be a great idea.

Karate. My crooked-tooth right-hand man. Communications and explosives expert. Cool under fire and in crises. He stayed on in the action for years after we had called it quits. He'd survived and seemingly come out of it well. He'd simply continued 'Business as Usual', as we used to joke about the SAS.

Epilogue

1986 was a low ebb for Frelimo. The Renamo raids, the loss of their leader Samora Machel in an air crash and the collapse of their economy were seriously damaging.

The entry of the Zimbabweans into the conflict halted the rot but didn't turn the tide. Renamo stayed true to the guerrilla war principles we had taught them and simply melted away into the bush. In fact they even took their action across the border into Zimbabwe and did considerable damage there.

In their ten-year involvement it is estimated the Zimbabwe military suffered over 1,000 casualties and lost countless weapons, vehicles and aircraft they couldn't replace. One estimate puts the cost to Zimbabwe at in excess of US$300 million.

It simply wasn't sustainable.

Mugabe didn't need Renamo or South Africa to destroy his own economy. He did it himself.

The conflict in Mozambique ebbed and flowed in the years that followed without either side ever coming close to a decisive victory.

Inevitably there was a serious decline in morale on both sides, but predominantly with Frelimo. Some Frelimo units were losing as many as thirty per cent of their men to desertion, most heading to Malawi to escape the deprivation.

Renamo fared better because of their strategy and South African support, but many were tired of conflict and wanted an end.

Convincing Frelimo leader Chissano, and Renamo leader Dhaklama, of the need for an end was a more difficult proposition, but eventually in 1990 they agreed to hold talks. They started in July and it took two years before there was a final agreement and peace. And in the interim Renamo didn't let up, keeping the pressure on Frelimo.

The country's first ever elections were held in October 1994. Chissano defeated Dhaklama in the presidential election, but Renamo was able to win 112 seats to Frelimo's 125 in the new parliament.

Peace eventually came to Mozambique.

The Assassination of Samora Machel?

Pig Dog, Karate and I were staying at the Mountain House, high up on the snow-covered slopes of Mount Taranaki in New Zealand. Karate had come to see us and this was our last morning with him. Outside a cold southerly wind had blown away the clouds, and the temperature was just a couple of degrees above freezing.

Sensibly we headed for the comfortable armchairs in front of the fire in the guest lounge.

'You will be the first to hear the story I'm about to tell you,' Karate said.

'The South African reaction to the killing of Dave Berry created serious distrust amongst the SAS who had joined the Recce Commando after Rhodesia, and most left not long after that.

'I felt that distrust as well but not as strongly because I was far away and buried in the Renamo campaign, but I'm very glad I did feel that way, because if I hadn't, I don't think I'd be here telling you this story.'

Pig Dog and I looked at him in astonishment.

'What do you mean by that?' asked Pig Dog.

'Are you suggesting the South Africans would have taken you out?'

'Exactly,' replied Karate.

'I knew too much. If I had revealed what I am about to tell you there would have been massive repercussions for South Africa, and I don't think they would have risked that.'

'You see I believe we were instrumental in the assassination of Frelimo leader Samora Machel.'

'My God!' I exclaimed. 'The plane crash. Don't tell me you were involved in that?'

'Not just involved,' said Karate. 'I think we caused it.'

'Who is we?' asked Pig Dog.

'What about the others. Have any of them been taken out?'

'No,' he replied. 'There was just one other involved. Edwin Chingadzi was ex-RAR and then joined the Selous Scouts. He was a sergeant and a great operator, also working with Renamo. I really enjoyed his company. He would have been good value in our SAS team.

'After the operation he resigned and headed for Cape Town. His plan was to shave off his beard, change his identity, and join his brother who ran a garage in the depths of the coloured area. He would be safe there.

'We were both back in Durban on R and R when we were summoned to the Colonel's office.

'He told us he had been approached for assistance with a special operation involving some new communication equipment. He wasn't sure what it was but suspected it was radio intercept gear that could eavesdrop on enemy communications.

'He said with my radio and signalling skills I was the perfect choice, and I just happened to be available. Edwin would go with me as an assistant and to help carry the gear to a site somewhere "up in the mountains".

'He told us the operation would take about a week, and then we would re-join our Renamo groups in southern Mozambique.

'The following day we were flown up to the SADF army and air base at Komatipoort, which sits on top of the Lebombo Mountains at the very southern end of the Kruger National Park. As our Renamo group progressed south we were supplied from this base, and I'd been there a couple of times when going in and out of R and R.

'At the base we were met by a couple of guys in plain clothes and taken to an office. I guess they were intelligence staff.

'In the office they produced what looked very similar to our usual TR28 HF radio, and as the Colonel had suggested they said it was a radio interceptor. It was very simple and used the same batteries as the HF radio. It just had one switch that turned it on and off.

'I asked about tuning and was told it operated on a small number of specially selected fixed frequencies and automatically flicked through them looking for radio traffic. If it found a signal it would lock on and transmit the traffic back to Komatipoort.

'It had an aerial – that again was not dissimilar to the standard G5RV we routinely used. They told us once we were in position, we were to put up the aerial and it should face Maputo – south-east from where we would be located.

'That afternoon Edwin and I packed the intercept gear, then we went to the local butcher's shop and bought several sticks of biltong. We added this and extra brew kit to our packs, and then realising we would be high in the mountains, and remembering the Angola operation where we took out the Luso camp, I went to the stores and got us a blanket each.'

Karate turned to look at me.

'"If you are warm you will sleep well, and if you sleep well, you'll work well," I seem to remember you telling us, Mick.'

We all laughed.

'Are you taking the piss out of me, Karate?' I threatened.

'Always,' he said and we laughed again.

'As it got dark, we were taken in a Land Rover that went south for just over one hundred kilometres towards the border with Swaziland.

'We were dropped off not far past a small settlement known as Mbuzini. From there we were to head due east and position ourselves somewhere in the rugged Lebombo Mountains that formed the border with Mozambique.

'That night we walked for about five hours towards the silhouetted mountain peaks. Happy we were well clear of any human settlement we bedded down for the night.

'Next day was hard work as we climbed deep into the mountain chain. Above us were great bare granite mounds while we worked our way through huge broken boulders with thick vegetation.

'Eventually we reached a place where we could see across the great plains of Mozambique. We settled into a cave between boulders. The cover was good and there was water nearby. We were secure. Nobody would find us.

'That afternoon we set up the radio and gave Komatipoort our location. We told them we had also rigged up the second radio and asked for instructions. We were given another sched time for the following day and that was all. Edwin and I made ourselves comfortable and enjoyed the view.

'The next day we were told to switch on the second radio at 2000 hours that night and we were to leave it on until midnight. We were told the battery would be flat by then and we'd need to change it. We had three spares with us.

'We switched the machine on as instructed at 2000 hours. A green LED illuminated to let us know it was on, and we went back to our blankets while it performed its silent magic.

'Edwin and I were both dozing when we suddenly heard the engine noise of a jet aircraft. At first, we didn't think anything of it as there were flights into Maputo that wasn't so far away.

'But it got louder and louder. I went to the edge of the cave and could see the navigation lights of what looked like a big plane heading directly towards us. It was low but cleared the granite peaks above us OK, then just as I was thinking it must be a flight into Swaziland there was a massive explosion and crashing.

'The plane had come down!

'Edwin was by now standing next to me. We were both stunned and unsure what to do or say, but then we looked down at the green LED that was still glowing strongly, and the sickening realisation suddenly dawned on us both.

'We didn't know for sure, but it looked like the two of us with this second radio were responsible for a plane crash.

'I leapt forward and immediately switched off the device.

'Edwin,' I said, 'there will soon be people swarming all over this area, and we can't trust the South Africans. If we are caught with this device guess who they will be blaming? Two rebel Renamo fighters. We need to get out of here as quickly as we can.'

'Bloody good thinking,' interjected Pig Dog.

'I agree,' I said. 'Getting out of there was a good move, but you can't say for sure that it was your device that somehow guided the aircraft into the mountainside. The circumstantial evidence is strong and I'll add to that by saying that your tasking was also very unusual. You don't need a couple of guys with a fancy new radio to do intercept work.

'When I was on Staff Course, we visited a couple of radio intercept sites and they both had big sophisticated equipment. The South Africans could have monitored anything transmitted in southern Mozambique from the safety of their base in Komatipoort.

'Sending you two out there doesn't make sense, however it doesn't prove that what you were doing had anything to do with the crash.'

'But, Mick, the plane flew directly towards us,' Karate objected.

'Yes,' I replied, 'but why did it fly into the mountain? What about altimeters and all the ground proximity warning devices aircraft have these days? Even if your radio did guide the plane in your direction it couldn't have interfered with that equipment.'

'Just doesn't make sense,' I added again.

'Yes. You're right, Mick,' said Karate, 'But that didn't change anything for us.

'The first thing we did was to bury the second radio and its aerial in the gravel at the back of the cave. We then packed up as quickly as we could and started the slow descent to the foot of the mountain range. It got easier as we got lower, and not long after midnight we were on the plains below.

'We headed north, keeping close to the base of the mountain range where there was cover for us and hopefully water.

'We kept going until just before four in the morning when we bedded down in thick cover.

'The sun was well up when we started again. We kept close to cover because I was afraid they might come looking for us by helicopter. As the morning progressed there was a lot of aircraft movement over the hills but none came anywhere near us.

'That afternoon I sent a signal to Komatipoort advising we had abandoned the mission and were on our way to re-join our Renamo group. I let them know the second radio had been disposed of. I didn't give them our location and told them I wouldn't be communicating again until I'd met up with Renamo.'

'Good one, Karate,' said Pig Dog. 'That would have put the cat amongst the pigeons.'

'We headed north until we eventually reached the Nkomati River which I knew joined the Sabi not far from where we were camped with Renamo. We shot a small antelope and a guineafowl along the way to supplement our rations. It took us eight days to meet up with Phillip and the gang.

'We told them we had been asked to recce the area to the south – didn't mention anything about the plane crash – but you can imagine our surprise and reaction when Phillip told us they had heard on the radio that Frelimo leader Samora Machel had been killed in a plane crash.

'Edwin and I just looked at each other. Getting the hell out of the area suddenly made even more sense than it did at the time, because we were sure it was us who had brought down the plane.

'When we had chance, we spoke about telling nobody and how we would quit the Recce Commando at the first available opportunity.

'Edwin made the first move. A couple of the South African boys with us were due out for R and R so Edwin jumped on board the chopper that went straight back to Durban. We didn't want to go anywhere near Komatipoort.

'He put in his resignation and told the Colonel that after the plane crash we were worried about compromise so we had decided to abandon the mission and head back to Renamo. Edwin told him we buried the equipment we were given at the back of a cave high in the mountains where it would never be found.

'He was happy about that and Edwin duly headed off to the Cape to join his brother.

'I decided I'd wait a bit longer just to see how things panned out. I stayed another month with Renamo. There wasn't much action; most of our time was spent training new recruits that were arriving on a daily basis, including an increasing number of Frelimo deserters who told us how they were being starved. There was very little food available and what little they were sent was hogged by their seniors.

'We had plenty of food and on top of that the South Africans kept on paying wages so it was no surprise that the recruits kept pouring into Renamo.

'I also managed to avoid Komatipoort and put in my resignation as soon as we reached Durban. I told the Colonel I'd done twelve years with the SAS, plus another six with them, and I'd had enough. I wanted to try a more normal life.

'As soon as I received my pay and pension money, I transferred it to my sister's account in Canada and bought a one-way ticket to London where my plan was to move around and make it impossible to be followed.

'I enjoyed myself in England for a few days then took the train to Paris. From there I flew to join my sister in Canada where I have been ever since.'

'Smart move,' said Pig Dog.

'Yes,' I said, 'you played it all bloody well, Karate, and what a story. My God, I'd love to know the truth about that second radio.'

'Mick,' he said, 'we'll never know, but in spite of your arguments I still believe that second radio somehow contributed to the plane crash.

'The fact that it killed Samora Machel doesn't bother me in the slightest, in fact it would have been bloody good news for many people in Mozambique given his orchestrated campaign of killing off the local chiefs and headmen.'

'Yes,' said Pig Dog. 'If it was your device that brought down the plane then you guys killed a terrorist leader. You'd get a medal for that in America!'

'But I don't think that would have saved our skin if we had been picked up by police or security forces,' replied Karate.

'It could all too easily have become another "unauthorised mission" like the Dave Berry story and I sure as hell wasn't going to let that happen.'

Can't argue with that!

The Undisputed Facts About the Tupolev Tu-134 Crash

The investigations that followed the crash revealed a number of facts about which there is also no argument:

The Tupolev Tu-134 is a medium range commercial twin-jet airliner capable of carrying up to eighty passengers plus flight and cabin crew.

It has a range of up to 3,000 km and a cruise speed of 900 km/hr.

The aircraft in question had a major inspection in Russia two years before the crash and subsequently had been properly serviced and maintained. Data from the flight recorder showed the aircraft and all its systems to be operating normally.

The all-Russian crew were operating the plane for the Mozambique government. They were experienced in flying in Mozambique and were well familiar with landing at Maputo airport where they were usually based.

On 19 October 1986, the aircraft had flown Samora Machel and his entourage to Mbala in north eastern Zambia, close to the border with Tanzania. At the end of a meeting with the Zambian president and others, it departed at 1838 hours for the return, non-stop trip back to Maputo.

The weather on route was fine and an ETA of 2125 hours was filed.

First contact with Maputo Air Traffic Control was at 2046 hours while the aircraft was cruising at 35,000 feet. The aircraft reported its position and confirmed it was flying towards the Maputo navigation beacon.

The next contact was at 2102 hours when the crew reported they were descending. Maputo acknowledged and asked them to check in again when they were at 3,000 feet or when they could see the runway lights. For the next eight minutes the plane maintained the required track and it was all business as usual.

At 2110 hours the usual changed to unusual and ultimately to catastrophic.

At 2110 hours the aircraft made a 37° turn to the right, away from Maputo.

On the cockpit voice recorder, the navigator stated the distance to Maputo was 100 km. This was followed by a comment from the captain about the turn, to which the navigator responded by saying the Maputo beacon indicated that way.

At 2115 hours the navigator stated the distance to Maputo was 60 km.

At 2118 hours the aircraft had descended to 3,000 feet; Maputo was advised. The descent continued and Air Traffic Control granted an 'Instrument Landing System' approach to runway 23.

The Tupolev crew reported that the ILS was out of service and also asked Maputo to check their runway lights.

At 2121 hours the navigator stated the distance to Maputo was 20 km and repeated the request for Maputo to check the runway landing lights. The captain said something was wrong. The co-pilot said the runway lights were not on.

At 2,600 feet the ground proximity warning system sounded. The captain cursed but continued the descent.

The Tupolev crashed into the Lebombo Mountains at an altitude of 2,185 feet killing 27 of the 35 passengers and crew on board, including Mozambique President and Frelimo leader Samora Machel.

The crash was first reported to the South African Police at Mbuzini at 2300 hours, and the first police to reach the crash site did so around forty minutes later.

The first medical people to reach the site did so around 0100 in the morning, with helicopters arriving as it got light three hours or so later to take the survivors to the nearest hospital which was at Nelspruit.

And at this point we leave the known truth because accounts of what happened next are murky, prejudiced, and in some cases downright lies.

The South African Response

Putting aside Karate's story and the other suggestions of sabotage that followed, this was a tricky situation for South Africa.

A communist Russian aircraft with Russian crew, carrying the communist Mozambique leader, had crashed inside South African territory. On the one hand, if one emphasises the 'communist' and 'enemy' aspects of this there would be cause for celebration.

The news certainly didn't bother Karate, and his Renamo mates were delighted. I recall my own reaction: it was a pity this couldn't also happen to people like Mugabe and Idi Amin in Uganda, and the more Russian planes that crashed the better.

Let's not forget we were still very much in Cold War times.

On the other hand, this was a civil aviation accident, so regardless of the aircraft origin, who it was carrying, and politics, ICAO international protocols demanded a professional and humane response.

The South Africans delivered this but along the way milked the situation to their own advantage and made a few bad mistakes that created distrust, which in a way vindicated the precautions Karate and Edwin took.

Foreign Minister Pik Botha for example, declared that autopsies of the Russian flight crew suggested they were intoxicated by alcohol and that the aircraft in question was an obsolete model. Both assertions were incorrect and he later admitted that what he said was aimed at deflecting the increasing criticism his country had to face in the aftermath of the crash.

The South African Police who first arrived on the scene were not slow to recognise this was an intelligence bonanza. Special teams were flown in to sift through the personal possessions, which included Samora Machel's briefcase. The police also secured the all-important cockpit voice recorder and the flight data recorder – the two 'black boxes' carried on the plane.

Amongst the many items of interest recovered were details of a plan to oust Malawi leader Dr Hastings Banda in a combined operation by Zimbabwe and Mozambique. Banda was despised because of his pragmatic approach to relations with South Africa, and his refusal to get involved with the debilitating regional conflicts going on around his small country.

Pik Botha was advised of the crash at around 0430 hours that morning by the Minister for Law and Order who advised that over thirty had been killed, including Samora Machel. Given the sensitivity of the situation Pik Botha agreed to meet Sergio Vieira, Mozambique Minister of Security, and together they travelled to the site where the body of Samora Machel was positively identified.

After the identification Vieira requested that documents taken from the site be handed over to him. The South Africans had already copied everything so immediately complied with his request.

In South Africa air accidents were the responsibility of the Department of Transport who set about forming a Board of Enquiry. They decided on appointing six members – three South Africans and three from the international community.

The three international members were Frank Borman from the USA – he was an engineer, test pilot, astronaut and then CEO of Eastern Airlines; Geoff Wilkinson, from the UK, who headed Britain's Air Accidents Investigation Branch; and finally Sir Edward Eveleigh, former Lord Justice of Appeal and member of the British Privy Council.

The three South Africans were Jan Germishuys, former South African Commissioner for Civil Aviation, Pieter van Hoven, who was then chairman of the South African Airlines Association, and finally the Board chairman, Cecil Margo, who was a member of the Supreme Court and had previous experience with air accident enquiries.

It was a high-powered Board whose experience and credibility could not be questioned.

Their credentials didn't stop it happening though, as Mozambique and other African states immediately cried 'Foul!' and accused the South Africans of murder.

The Board Findings

The Board concluded it was probable the flight crew had unwittingly set one of the two on-board navigation beacons to the frequency of the guidance beacon at Matsapa Airport in Swaziland, on the other side of the Lebombo Mountains.

They believed the error came about because of poor instrument design, including a lack of back lighting, combined with the fact that the frequencies for Maputo and Matsapa were very close to each other. Maputo operated on 112.7 MHz, Matsapa on 112.3 MHz.

The navigator made the fatal 37° turn believing he was on the Maputo frequency when in fact he was following the beacon at Matsapa Airport.

Looking at the map and where the turn was made, the adjusted flight path heads directly for Matsapa.

The Board were critical of the fact that the captain and crew incorrectly assumed Maputo airport had an electrical blackout, when throughout the descent they had radio contact with Air Traffic Control, who therefore must have had power, and the fact that back-up generators for navigational equipment was a standard requirement for airports.

Finally, the Board concluded that if the flight crew had performed the required procedures in response to a ground proximity warning, even just seconds before impact, the crash would have been prevented.

The findings of the Board were signed off by all six members and presented to the South African Minister of Transport on 2 July 1987, and in accordance with international convention copies were sent to Mozambique and to Russia – the manufacturer of the aircraft.

The Mozambique Response

The authorities in Mozambique knew something was wrong when the presidential plane didn't arrive after reporting to Maputo that it was at 3,000 feet, but it was only at 0650 hours the following morning when the South African government let them know an aircraft bound for Maputo had crashed into mountains inside their border.

Funeral music played on national radio through the day and later Frelimo made a broadcast announcing the president's death. It said the crash was a criminal act but did not directly accuse South Africa.

They made several submissions in response to the Board report, and commissioned an experienced investigator from the New Zealand Office of Air Accidents to look at the possibility of tampering or replacing the genuine Maputo beacon with a decoy. He concluded it would not be difficult to set up a mobile beacon, but pointed out that for it to work the genuine beacon in Maputo would have to be turned off.

In spite of this they stated that new evidence from Russia suggested the aircraft turned to follow a false signal, and that the actions of the Maputo Air Traffic Controller and flight crew were not the main causes of the accident.

Mozambique was in denial.

The Russian Response

The Russians endorsed the factual information contained in the report but challenged the findings, stating that the reasons for the 37° turn remained unresolved, and they totally rejected the criticism of the crew's actions.

They went on to claim that the signal from the Matsapa beacon was not strong enough at the point of the turn for their navigational equipment to receive it, and it could not therefore have been the cause of the deviation.

They concluded that the aircraft's equipment performed with the required accuracy for a safe flight.

They said the crew's qualifications and experience excluded the possibility that the deviation was a result of their unpreparedness or inattentiveness. They claimed the crew were efficient in monitoring the aircraft and in maintaining contact with Maputo Air Traffic Control.

They said the signal that lured the aircraft into the mountain was the result of a premeditated action.

The Russians, predictably, were in a more aggressive denial.

South Africa does the Right Thing

In response to the allegations from Russia and Mozambique the South Africans then undertook a series of test flights to determine if it was indeed possible to pick up the beacon signal from Matsapa when on the final approaches to Maputo.

Both military and commercial aircraft were used in the experiment and all confirmed receiving the signal from Matsapa.

It didn't convince Russia or Mozambique because they simply didn't want to know.

Commenting on this reaction the Portuguese journalist José Milhazes made the valid point that both the Soviet and Mozambique authorities had an interest in spreading the thesis of sabotage by the South African government. The Soviets wanted to safeguard their reputation by exonerating their flight crew, while the Mozambique Frelimo party wanted to make their fallen leader a hero.

Samora Machel will never be a hero in my eyes.

To me he was a Marxist-Leninist extremist and a terrorist leader. Mozambique was better off for him being dead.

During our SAS operations in Mozambique and Angola I saw too much callous and barbaric brutality against the local populations to feel any other way about people like Frelimo's Samora Machel and MPLA's Holden Roberto.

To me they were irrational, power hungry dictators who in spite of their rhetoric actually didn't give a toss about their people. It was all about them. Same for Mugabe. Same for Amin.

If there were any heroes, they would be Karate and Edwin.

In later years I tagged along with the New Zealand delegation to an ICAO security conference held in Jakarta. I met members of the American FAA as well as British and Australian security representatives. I asked them all about the possibility of a decoy beacon and got the same answer from everyone.

'Yes, it was possible to rig up a mobile guidance beacon,' they all said, 'but it would need a couple of big trucks. One for the power generator and another for the guidance equipment, and for it to work the beacon being replaced would have to be switched off or totally incapacitated. It's the sort of scenario that could happen if there was a natural disaster for example.'

But such calm logical rationale was not available to our two heroes sitting in a cave in the Lebombo Mountains on the night of the crash.

Karate immediately went into survival mode.

They got rid of what they thought might be incriminating evidence and then disappeared into the African bush.

That's what we did.

That was SAS.

The Grahams of Burnley

The Graham family of Burnley had no tradition of military service on either the maternal or the paternal sides, yet in spite of this three successive generations managed to get embroiled in war.

All three generations managed to survive intact, although they all had close shaves with death.

All three lived into their seventies, and all three died of lung cancer.

Grandpa

Born in 1898 Private Frederick Graham worked in one of Burnley's cotton mills before enlisting with the East Lancashire Regiment during the First World War.

Grandpa's war was at Ypres in Belgium where in five separate battles somewhere between 800,000 and one million soldiers lost their lives. It is a miracle therefore that he survived, but he didn't escape unscathed.

His first experience was to be buried alive.

They were charging the German lines when suddenly there was no ground beneath his feet. With mud everywhere the shell hole full of liquid mud was invisible and he fell into the middle of it. He was completely submerged in the mire and could not swim. Somehow he clawed his way to the edge and was dragged out by retreating comrades.

Having recovered from that ordeal he was then caught in the middle of a mustard gas attack. He was ill for a few days but was soon back in action.

If it were not for he and his close friend deciding to disobey orders he would have lost his life in the next incident.

Before a bayonet charge, soldiers were routinely required to unload their Leigh-Enfield rifles. Given the casualty rate of this war it's hard to imagine anyone thinking of such a 'safety' measure, but they did and that was the requirement.

Grandpa, however, told me they used to pretend to unload but didn't – instead the two of them kept a round in the breach ready for firing.

They charged the German lines and this time they reached them. He lunged at a German soldier in the trench in front of him with his bayonet, but instead of impaling the man he slipped in the mud and fell flat on his back.

Seeing his chance, the German raised his own bayonet above his head to make the fatal strike. As his arms stretched above his head my grandfather fired, hitting the man in the throat.

As the German staggered backwards from the impact of the shot, the rifle and bayonet dropped towards Grandpa, who was still lying on the ground. The bayonet sliced through his calf muscle and embedded itself in the ground.

He pulled it out and with help from his friend limped back to their own lines where his wound was treated by the medics.

His final act of the war earned him an 'MID' – mention in despatches. MIDs are awarded for acts of bravery that don't quite meet the criteria for the bigger medals.

They were retreating from yet another unsuccessful bayonet charge at the German lines. He was half way back when he stumbled across a badly wounded man lying in the mud. He picked up the man and put him across his shoulders.

As he staggered towards the safety of their trenches, he was caught in a German artillery barrage. Ignoring the blasts and shrapnel he continued doggedly on. As he reached the edge of the trenches the blast of an exploding shell blew him and the wounded man over and into safety.

The wounded man turned out to be a captain in an artillery regiment, and managed to survive his ordeal. After the war my grandparents moved to the village of Heysham at the southern end of Morecambe Bay, and were visited regularly over the following years by the man whose life he saved.

Grandpa was a heavy smoker all his life. Players and Woodbines were the brands he smoked. Looking back through old family photographs there are very few where he hasn't a burning cigarette between his fingers.

He died of lung cancer in the spring of 1976. I took some leave from the SAS and managed to reach him two days before the end.

Kids generally love their grandparents, and I was no exception. Grandpa and I shared some special times walking Morecambe Bay when the tide was out. I'd help him collect drift wood for their fire, while at the same time watching the prolific birdlife that fed in the soft sand and muddy tidal channels.

The calls of oystercatchers, curlews and redshanks filled the air while a biting wind off the Irish Sea made my eyes water and my nose run, but I was with him and to me it was magic.

It broke my heart when he died.

Father

Born in Burnley in 1920, Flight Sergeant Frederick Walter Graham was the only son of Beatrice and Frederick – my grandparents.

After school he completed a City and Guilds apprenticeship in woodwork. He was very skilled, to the extent that in later years he earned useful extra income through his ability to repair or recreate parts for damaged antique furniture.

The Second World War was already in progress when his apprenticeship was completed, and in late 1940 he volunteered to join the Royal Air Force. There was an excitement about aircraft, and while he had no illusions about the risks involved, he figured it had to be better than what his father went through in the army at Ypres.

He was trained at a number of bases during that year and thrived in the environment. The RAF found a talent for navigation and he later combined that with bomb aiming. He was promoted to Flight Sergeant and posted to one of the newly formed 'Pathfinder' Lancaster bomber squadrons.

Before going into action, he married Joan, his school days sweetheart, a marriage that would last for 55 years.

From 1942 he was on continuous active service, his squadron marking targets in Germany with incendiary flares ahead of the main bombing waves.

In late summer 1942 his squadron was tasked with marking the German railway factories at Mannheim. Trains and the railway network were critical to the German war effort, particularly their plans to invade Russia, so were strategic targets for the RAF bombers.

Unsurprisingly they were well defended and Dad's Lancaster was hit by flak. One of the starboard engines was dead and the aircraft was badly damaged, but all the crew were OK and the plane was still flying.

They were limping back to base and had the English Channel in sight when they were spotted by German escort fighters returning to base. With an easy kill in the offing they attacked the crippled Lancaster.

My father managed to leap from the burning aircraft and parachuted to safety. The plane exploded moments after his jump, and he was the only crew member to survive.

He landed safely but was handed over to the Germans by sympathetic Vichy French, and was interned in various PoW camps for the next two and a half years.

On repatriation he attended Chester College and ultimately qualified as a teacher. He was determined to bring up his family as far away from war-torn Europe as possible and the family ended up in Rhodesia – now Zimbabwe.

He was one of the staff at an agricultural college known as 'Domboshawa', and his job was to teach three hundred African students everything about wood and woodworking. It was an ideal situation in that it combined his apprenticeship skill with the newly acquired teaching qualification.

Dad started smoking while in the RAF and continued for the rest of his life.

Life in Rhodesia encouraged smoking. The country produced the finest Virginia tobacco in the world and cigarettes were cheap; a packet of fifty Matinée – his brand – cost just two shillings and sixpence.

The packets of fifty cigarettes were known as 'The Rhodesian Notebook' because the back of the pack was plain white, ideal for taking notes. All Rhodesian males carried them in their top left shirt pocket with a pen or pencil clipped next to the cigarettes.

My mother didn't smoke but most Rhodesian women did.

In the end smoking killed my father, and while I managed to see Grandpa at the end, I missed my father by a day. He died while I was on board a Qantas flight heading to Africa. My brother had called saying he'd been given six weeks. I booked on the first available flight but was too late because he only lasted six days. He was 76.

The Author

Born in Burnley on 10 March 1946, Major Michael Frederick Graham retired as Second-in-Command of C Squadron (Rhodesian) Special Air Service.

My introduction to the military was at Easter in 1967 when, home from university, my father gave me a letter from the Rhodesian Ministry of Defence. It contained my call-up papers for nine months national service.

'I think you will find this the best education you've had so far,' I remember him telling me, and he was right. To me officer training was far more interesting than the dry university business of looking at dusty old bones from one animal or another (I had studied zoology).

And it didn't stop there. Three years on there was Platoon Commanders Course, three years after that Company Commanders Course, and ultimately Staff College, that in terms of intensity and quality of content would surpass the high-pressure MBA courses that became very popular with those making a career in business.

I met the SAS for the first time during officer training. It was the only time in the twelve years that followed that an SAS detachment assisted the School of Infantry with training. I got to know a couple of the men reasonably well while they were there and they convinced me the SAS was where I wanted to be.

I passed the SAS Selection Course a year later and was on continuous active service thereafter.

SAS Selection Course was hard but didn't trouble me. I'd trained hard for a month beforehand in the mountains of the Eastern Highlands, but looking back it was also because since the age of 11 I'd been building up a stamina base.

At primary school a teacher who loved running took a group of 11- and 12-year-olds out with him. During the holidays I kept it up by running around the six thousand acres of farmland where we lived.

In my first two years at high school I won my age group cross-country run and broke the school record both times.

As I got older, I got heavier and while still enjoying a long run I was no longer competitive, but in compensation I got faster over short distances and made the 440 yards my speciality. There were three or four lads faster than me in the country, but I was very happy to once go under 50 seconds at a local athletics meeting.

In 1964 I won the annual Que Que to Umvuma road walk – twenty-six miles, and much later on my 31st birthday in March 1977, I ran the Rhodes Athletic Club marathon in three and a quarter hours with another five SAS men.

I mention all this because how can a non-smoker with an athletic background and a later life of good diet and plenty of exercise suddenly be stricken with an incurable, untreatable form of lung cancer?

It doesn't stack up, but that's what happened. And to rub salt in the wound the two heavy smokers before me both lived three years longer than I will.

It is what it is.

C'est la vie!